Bill McLaren's
DREAM LIONS

BILL McLAREN

with additional contributions from
WILLIE JOHN McBRIDE
and **IAN McGEECHAN**

PHOTOGRAPHS BY COLORSPORT

CollinsWillow
An Imprint of HarperCollins*Publishers*

First published in 1998 by Collins Willow
an imprint of HarperCollinsPublishers
London

© Lennard Associates Ltd 1998

1 3 5 7 9 8 6 4 2

A CIP catalogue record for this book is available from the British Library

ISBN 0 00 218861 9

Produced by Lennard Books
a division of Lennard Associates Ltd
Mackerye End
Harpenden
Herts AL5 5DR

Production editor Ian Osborn
Editor Kirsty Ennever
Jacket design by Paul Cooper Design
Additional photographs by Peter Bush and *Rugby World*
Origination by The Colour Edge

Printed and bound in Great Britain
by Butler & Tanner

CONTENTS

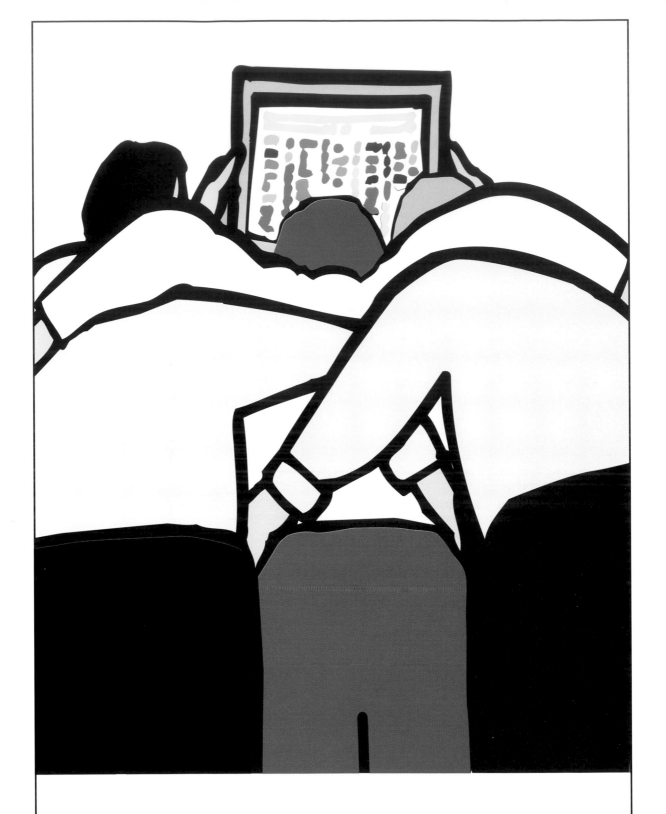

When it comes to passing information, we're in front of the pack.

REUTERS

FOREWORD

A group of people will nearly always boast star individuals – but it's teamwork that really counts. The *Dream Lions* is crammed full of individuals with undoubted outstanding talent, but these individuals need support from their team-mates.

It's a scenario that isn't too far removed from life at Reuters. Not only are we the world's leading information provider – including sports information – we are considered to be the best.

We monitor over 50 sports worldwide and publish at least 100 sports stories daily. A recent innovation is the Reuters SportsWeb (www.sportsweb.com), an internet site which provides up-to-the-minute international sports news and pictures from around the world.

To be the best, we too employ outstanding people – but their innovative ideas and actions would count for little if they didn't have the necessary back-up of their colleagues.

Coaching individuals to be part of a team is also essential. This book contains a chapter by Ian McGeechan – who coached last years (real) Lions during their triumphant tour of South Africa – on how he would coach the Dream Lions.

He talks of mental strength and individual brilliance – attributes which are now essential to play a whole team game.

I, for one, wouldn't argue with that!

JULIE HOLLAND
Managing Director
Reuters UK & Ireland

great performers

Scottish Life

the **PENSION** company

Good training, excellent teamwork, outstanding results – they've all combined to win us five-star service awards for four years running. A great performance from our own 'Dream Team'.

FOREWORD

Having been born and brought up in Hawick, rugby football almost inevitably became an indelible part of my life from an early age. And Bill McLaren has been an intrinsic element of my 'rugby life' ever since.

During the post-war era when I was growing up, Bill was a Hawick stalwart who, had it not been for illness, would surely have represented his country as well as his town.

But it was not just as a player that Bill's influence was felt. In many respects, he made a much greater contribution to the game through his role as a primary school teacher in Hawick. His gift as an educationalist extended to teaching eager and aspiring young schoolboys the rudiments of rugby and instilling into them the traditions and passion of the game as it pertained to Hawick.

I had the personal misfortune to pass through what would normally have been Bill McLaren's primary school sphere of influence at the time he was recovering from the effects of a tuberculosis attack. However, I'm not sure Bill ever realised I wasn't in his classes at school since, when introducing me to his media colleagues, he has often referred to me as one of his 'boys'. I've much preferred being thought of in that light than publicly contradicting the great man.

In spite of all the rugby 'greats' that he is known to personally, and the thousands of others that he has met over the years and throughout the world, he has retained a close interest in anything to do with rugby in his native Hawick. So it was typical of the man that, in bumping into me at Heathrow Airport after a gap of several years, he was able to link me to the junior team, The Trades, that I had played for in Hawick many years previously.

With this background, it's hardly surprising that when the opportunity became available for myself and the Scottish Life to be associated with this publication, the decision was not a difficult one to make. It is probably already apparent that I'm a frustrated rugby player. Although it may be a bit difficult to imagine in today's environment, the initial ambition of a young male Teri (a native of Hawick) was to play for 'The Greens'. That club has had an illustrious history with a long list of international players and others, such as Bill, who have made their name in different aspects of the great game.

Bill's commentating skills and his attention to detail, combined with his perceptive and warm personality, and the incomparable range of rugby matches of the highest quality which he has witnessed, put him in a unique position to contemplate selecting the 'dream team' of his era. And given the quality of his views, his selection will command respect.

It is a great honour to be associated with this book. I am sure it will bring much pleasure, as well as considerable opportunity for debate, to rugby folk across the world.

MALCOLM MURRAY
Chief General Manager
The Scottish Life Assurance Company

Glenfiddich®

In a league of its own and the world's favourite single malt whisky

Over a 100 years since the first Glenfiddich ran from its stills, the Glenfiddich Distillery remains faithful to its traditional methods of whisky production, ensuring that the unique character of Glenfiddich is not compromised in any way.

For the maximum enjoyment, drink Glenfiddich neat or cut with a little water or ice.

INTRODUCTION
by
Willie John McBride

British Lions' tours changed for ever in 1971, when the Lions won a series for the very first time. That was the dawn of a whole new era which has resulted in the Lions winning four of the eight Test series on the tours made between 1971 and 1997.

Those Lions' victories were achieved in 1971 in New Zealand, in 1974 and 1997 in South Africa and in 1987 in Australia. There is no doubt that this quarter of a century has been the golden period of British Lions' rugby. Of the tours before 1971, the only one on which the Lions really distinguished themselves was in 1955, when the series against South Africa was shared, two Tests each.

I was well aware as we flew to New Zealand in 1971 that British Lions had not done very well in the 1960s as I had been a member of all three tours – in 1962 and 1968 to South Africa and in 1966 to New Zealand. We played four Tests on each of those tours and, to put it kindly, our record was not very impressive. We drew the first Test in which I didn't play in 1962 in South Africa but lost the other three. In 1966 in New Zealand we suffered a whitewash, losing all four Tests, while back in South Africa in 1968 we drew the second Test in Port Elizabeth but lost the other three.

So when we landed in Auckland in 1971 at the start of a five month tour I was able to look back in dismay at my previous three tours: that record showed that I had managed one draw and eight defeats in my nine Tests for the Lions.

However, 1971 proved to be a turning point for Lions' rugby. When I look at the calibre of players we had on that tour, it is not a major surprise that we made history by becoming the only British Lions ever to win a Test series against New Zealand. I still get a warm glow every time I think of our Test back division on that trip and I recall all the heroics they performed throughout the 26 matches.

The fact that they are all still household names 27 years later speaks for itself. At full back we had the greatest defensive player in my era or any other era – J.P.R. Williams. He wasn't bad in attack either and was invaluable thundering in to the line to make the extra man and create the overlap or to counter-attack from full back when the opposition took the risk of kicking the ball in his direction. In 10 years I can't remember him ever dropping an opposition up and under.

We were also blessed on that tour with two of the most talented and exciting wings that the game has ever produced. On the right wing we had the quicksilver, elusive Gerald Davies. He was blisteringly fast and had the most wicked side-step I have ever seen. One unforgettable highlight was the day Gerald scored four sensational tries against Hawke's Bay.

On the left wing we had the power, the pace and the grace of David Duckham. He was a wonderfully balanced runner who played the best rugby of his career in New Zealand in 1971. He was a world-class player who rewrote the record books when he scored six fantastic tries against West Coast and Buller.

In the centre there was the perfect combination of the utterly dependable John Dawes and the multi-talented Mike Gibson, who was one of the most complete footballers Irish rugby has ever produced. Both these players always seemed to be in the right place and they invariably did the right thing. They had tremendous insight and were great readers of the game.

The other two members of our back division were quite simply the greatest pair of half backs ever to tour New Zealand. It is impossible to exaggerate the contribution made by the legendary Gareth Edwards and Barry John. Both were inspirational players who gave confidence to the whole team. These two geniuses completed one of the greatest back divisions ever to play rugby and it is easy to understand how six of the seven have made the Dream Team. Only John Dawes has missed out, to the brilliant attacking skills of Jeremy Guscott.

People often ask me how these outstanding players would have fared in the modern game. I can only say that they all had such fantastic skill and natural instinctive ability that I firmly believe they would all have been truly great players in any era.

Our forwards were also pretty good on that tour but it was an even better pack in 1974 when we enjoyed the most successful British Lions' tour ever. We were unbeaten in 22 matches in South Africa, winning 21 (including the first three Tests) and drawing the last Test. It was a fabulous four-month romp in which the forwards laid the foundations of our string of victories but we also had a top-class back division. We had Gareth Edwards and Phil Bennett at half-back with J.P.R. Williams at full-back, Andy Irvine and J.J. Williams on the wings and Ian McGeechan and Dick Milliken in the centre.

I was very privileged to be captain of the 1974 Lions and it was a sheer pleasure to be part of such a great touring party. No touring team in history has had a better record in South Africa than our Lions in 1974.

From that team, five forwards have made the Dream Team. In the front row Fran Cotton was an automatic selection at loose-head prop although he was the only front row forward I have ever come

across who was just as effective at tight-head prop. Both locks, myself and Gordon Brown, squeeze in to the Dream Team and so in the back row do Mervyn Davies at number eight and Fergus Slattery at open side flanker.

The other places in the Dream Team pack go to Peter Wheeler at hooker, Graham Price at prop and Mike Teague, the hero of the triumphant 1989 Lions' tour to Australia, at blind side flanker. I reckon that pack would get us enough ball to allow our collection of stars in the backs to win most matches.

I had enormous fun and fulfilment over a great many years playing international rugby for Ireland and I wouldn't have missed a minute of it for the world. But in the final analysis I have to say that the ultimate challenge and the ultimate thrill was to go on a British Lions' tour. My abiding memories will be drawing the fourth Test in Auckland to clinch the series against New Zealand and winning the third Test in Port Elizabeth to take an unbeatable three-Tests-to-none lead in the series against South Africa.

If I had one rugby wish for the future, apart from the occasional Triple Crown for Ireland, it would be the earnest plea that the concept of British Lions is never allowed to die.

The new professional game has put an in-house claustrophobic pressure on the domestic season with league matches starting nowadays in the middle of August and going on to the middle of May. That scarcely leaves time for a British Lions' tour even in its new abbreviated form of just 13 matches in eight weeks. But I believe these tours must be allowed to continue.

I know that anyone who, like me, was in Cape Town on 21 June 1997 to watch Matt Dawson score that magical try down the blind side, courtesy of an outrageous dummy to tie up the first Test for the Lions; or who, like me, was in Durban on 28 June to watch Jeremy Guscott drop that magnificent goal to win the second Test, will hope and pray that we will be given the opportunity of supporting the British Lions again in New Zealand, South Africa and Australia.

I just hope that in 25 years time I am able to walk into a bookshop and buy a copy of a book called *Dream Lions – 2000–2023*, the story of the best team from the first eight Lions' tours of the next millennium. And I just hope that all the players who go on all those Lions' tours have as much fun and enjoyment and pleasure from theirs as I had from mine.

1971. Willie John McBride (middle row, second from left) with the squad that toured New Zealand.

It's good to listen.

MEMORIES OF THE LIONS

It was John Macdonald Bannerman, a formidable Scot as sportsman and politician, who said of elusive success that it is a long road that appears to have no turning. Few would be inclined to disagree with the great man, a double peer, so to speak, not only among Scottish forwards of his generation but also when elevated to the House of Lords. Certainly not we Border folk.

Alas, Lord Bannerman, once Scotland's most capped player, late of Shawlands Academy and Glasgow HSFP, died a year or so before he could applaud the 1971 Lions. Ever since that remarkable tour of New Zealand, tongues have wagged about the feats of this grand crew, the first Lions' team to win an international series in the Land of the Long White Cloud. It would also be apposite to remember that the opening match – in Brisbane against Queensland – on that trip was lost. Four penalty goals beat a goal and two penalty goals. What a shame present-day scoring values were not in force: had they been, the Lions would have won.

No matter. Later, in helping to hurl a mighty spanner into the well-oiled machinery of All Black rugby, John Dawes, the captain and supreme passer of the ball, succeeded where his Lions' predecessors in New Zealand of 1904, 1908 (an Anglo-Welsh selection), 1930, 1950, 1959 and 1966 had failed. Bannerman, a past president of the Scottish Rugby Union and a proud stickler for the game's traditions, also marched with the times. In this instance he would have cheered, long and loud.

Why? Not least because the seeds of overall victory on that historic tour were

sown by the forwards – Willie John McBride, Delme Thomas, Gordon Brown, Ian McLauchlan, Sean Lynch, John Pullin, Peter Dixon, John Taylor, Derek Quinnell, Mervyn Davies and Fergus Slattery. Their unstinting work allowed the most talented of back divisions to display their magic – and if the conjurers were Barry John and Gareth Edwards at half-back, the conductor had to be the late Carwyn James, a coach the like of whom British rugby has rarely, if ever, seen, before or since.

Little wonder, therefore, that Gerald Davies, David Duckham, Mike Gibson, J.P.R. Williams and Dawes required no second bidding to apply their skills in the most intense of series which the Lions, having lost in Christchurch and drawn in Auckland, won 2-1. Dr Douglas William Cumming Smith, a large wing-threequarter and an Aberdonian we Scots sent to cure the many medical ills down South, was the forthright manager. He was also, it seems, blessed with second sight. Dr Smith predicted a 2-1 series win for the Lions *before* they left London.

I recollect, having been present in New Zealand in spirit only, one accompanying journalist describing the outcome of the tour as British rugby's 'Four Minute Mile': that elusive barrier finally thrust aside by a combination of high skill, total commitment, a touch of good fortune and sheer bloody-mindedness. As I wrote in my book *Talking of Rugby*, nostalgia can be beautiful.

It is no coincidence, of that I am convinced, that the triumphant trek around South Africa three years later had its roots in the events of 1971. The other prime factor had to be the presence of some substantial healthy specimens from the tour party who had so disturbed New Zealand's equilibrium. The captain this time was Willie John, a man it took generations to make. I admit to borrowing those latter words, a quotation about another giant of our times, I believe. In all other respects, the opinions are mine. Let there be no misunderstanding: my admiration for the unbeaten 1974 Lions knows few bounds.

Unlike some commentators, I am not interested in attempting to assess whether the 1974 trampling of South African rugby reputations by the British and Irish Lions was a greater accomplishment than the Everest scaling of 1971, if my deliberate lapse of geography is permitted. That a few base camps were destroyed on the way, I have no doubts ... Before retirement, perhaps I should remind readers that my day job in Hawick was that of schoolmaster. Media duties, electronic and written, have been a second string to the McLaren bow.

Willie John's principal aides this time round included several of his outstanding 1971 colleagues: JPR, Edwards, Mervyn Davies, Slattery, Brown, Sandy

Carmichael. There was also a canny young Scot by the name of Andrew Robertson Irvine, who had vast sections of rugby devotees, male and female, queuing for his autograph. Little wonder Syd Millar, the coach (though quaintly described in official tour schedules prepared by the Home Unions as the 'assistant manager'), found room for Irvine in two of the four series matches.

During their travels the Lions beat many records: 729 points, the most ever scored by a touring team in South Africa (with the help of the four-point try); 107 tries, the most scored by any Lions' team there; 79 points in four internationals, the most by any country in a series against the Springboks; the 28-9 win in the second international brought South Africa their heaviest defeat by any country. I would add that Irvine's 156 points for the tour set a new peak for the Lions' players; further, Brown's eight tries were the most by a forward on a tour of South Africa, who salvaged a modicum of self-respect when drawing the final international. Did Slattery score late on, to make it 22 wins out of 22? Perhaps.

As all this happened some 25 years ago, it is not disloyal (is it?) to ask, too, whether Roger Uttley – what a tour he had! – was correctly awarded his first-half try as the valiant Lions sought to condemn the Springboks to a whitewash series. Mind you, Uttley's appearance on the blindside flank in the internationals was a masterly stroke. Ostensibly a lock, it took the bemused South Africans until that final game to appreciate that the big man, though a veritable rock, was not exactly a gazelle in the speed stakes. Talk about an epic epoch.

All of which makes the 1977 tour of New Zealand so disappointing. Irvine (11 tries) and Graham Price, the Hercules at tight-head, apart, few reputations were enhanced on a depressing trip which, initially, had promised so much. Dawes, the hero of

1971, was coach and, make no mistake, got the players he wanted. In the circumstances, even with hindsight, it is difficult to explain why the series was lost 3-1. What was so galling was that the Lions commanded in 21 of their 25 matches and even at Eden Park in the last match were ahead until the closing minutes.

John Brooks, the amiable chief rugby writer of the *Christchurch Press* (where the Lions won, unlike in 1971), summed up matters succinctly when observing: 'The 1971 blueprint was left at home and there were dented reputations in the visiting camp. With a few exceptions, they did not rate as an entertaining side.'

I would like to think that the eminently fair Brooks, when reflecting on the exceptions, did have William Blackledge Beaumont in mind. He arrived in New Zealand as a replacement, got into the international side as Brown's partner at lock and at all times was as competent as he was hard-working. In later years I got to know Bill extremely well, finding him thorough, honest, sincere and the most loyal of friends and colleagues. The burly Hawick forwards of my youth would have approved, just a wee bit.

Bill, the honest broker of lock forwards, was in charge in 1980 in South Africa, another of those touch-and-go series which could have gone either way in the four internationals. But it has to be said that in losing 3-1, Beaumont's injury-stricken Lions had to run the gauntlet of constant comparison with the McBride victory machine of 1974.

Here again, the (1980) pack – Price, Peter Wheeler, Clive Williams, Beaumont, Maurice Colclough, John O'Driscoll, Derek Quinnell and Jeff Squire – ruled. The burden of eight replacements and continuing difficulties at half-back because of injuries would have sunk most teams. While in one sense British strength in depth was well illustrated, capped by an encouraging victory in the last

international, it was all too little, too late.

At least, though, there were worthy days of achievement in 1980 – in sharp contrast to a continuing downward spiral three years later in New Zealand. Willie John, a folk hero on a par with Colin Meads in those parts, was manager, Jim Telfer was coach and Ciaran Fitzgerald captain. For a variety of reasons it was not a winning combination. If, as I wrote at length in *Talking of Rugby*, I repeat that Colin Deans – yes, he is from Hawick – would be my first choice hooker in McLaren's Best Northern Hemisphere XV, I imply no disrespect to Fitzgerald. Indeed, I have always valued his contributions as Ireland captain and as a co-commentator. It is just that Deans, the reserve hooker in 1983, was the better player: simple as that.

The Lions were never going to drop their captain, a factor (though not a fact, of course) that John Mason, an old friend at *The Daily Telegraph*, now retired, has politely stressed through the years. But even he must surely agree that in the testing matches on that difficult tour, the Lions, who lost all four internationals, started at a disadvantage, not least with the throwing at the line out.

Few will forget the humiliations of the 38-6 farewell defeat at Eden Park or, come to that, the five other losses. I am certain Telfer bears the scars to this day. There were squabbles, too, among the tour party, one of which ended in a bloody scrap at the back of the squad bus. Such a waste, such feeling. Those involved would have been better off enjoying a 'sook' at a Hawick Ball, those mint sweets I always carry in my briefcase.

There was no tour in 1986 as South Africa, wrongly in my view, bowed to outside political pressures and decided not to invite the Home Unions. So it was 1989 before the renowned red jersey and its impressive badge were taken into battle again. This time the destination was Australia, whose rapid advance in world rankings, beginning in 1984, permitted them to be sole hosts of a Lions' tour for the first time. Scotland's Finlay Calder was captain, a forthright back-row forward who, to my knowledge, could provide an amalgam of fun-poking, often at himself, and reasoned judgement. The management team comprised the talkative Clive Rowlands, for whom *calon*, the Welsh for heart, was the key, the admirable Ian McGeechan and Uttley, the steadfast flanker in the heroics of 1974 and back on Lions' duty as assistant coach.

Bearing in mind what happened in Sydney first time round, the Lions did mightily well to take the series 2-1. The 30-12 defeat in the opening international had the Lions on the back foot, if not on their backsides. Ironically a slip by David Campese allowed Ieuan Evans to poach the try that ultimately turned things round: 19-12 in Brisbane, 19-18 in Sydney, to the Lions.

The 13-match tour of New Zealand in 1993 provided ample ammunition for those who believe in the old tag about meeting triumph and disaster, 'And treat those two impostors just the same', as Kipling put it. It was so very close for the Lions, who on the important occasions owed so much to Gavin Hastings, an inspirational captain. No Scottish bias there, not least because some others in the tour party, my 'ain folk', were rather less successful. It is best to draw a veil over the activities of the mid-week team, especially in the final fortnight.

The industrious Gavin led by example. It was not just his goal-kicking, no matter that he scored 38 of the 51 points in the three internationals, which included a 20-7 win at Athletic Park, Wellington. At all times, even when it seemed that he might miss the Wellington match because of injury, Hastings was the man of the tour. He would not allow heads to go down, or controversy to simmer, even when a late, late penalty award in the opening international in Christchurch

went against the Lions. Grant Fox kicked the goal that made it a victory, 20-18, to the All Blacks: Fox, five penalty goals, Hastings six.

There were only two Lions' tries in the series – Rory Underwood in Wellington, Scott Gibbs in Auckland – as against five by New Zealand, but there were several bonuses, including the emergence of Ben Clarke, lately of Bishop's Stortford. The New Zealanders were so impressed by his back row skills (all three positions) that he was voted one of the Five Players of the Year. Not a unique honour but, nevertheless, one only rarely awarded to a Northern Hemisphere player.

While this is one of the few distinctions that have eluded Jeremy Guscott, that prince of English centres, he has for all that written his name large in the history of British rugby union, the greatest team game I know. Just as he had done with a solo try against the Wallabies at a critical time in 1989, so Guscott repeated the most memorable of thrusts in 1997. This time it was a drop goal, the score that won the match and the series 2-1: Saturday, 18 June 1997, King's Park, Durban, four minutes remaining, the Lions having existed on barely 30 per cent possession.

Whisper it very quietly but at that stage the Springboks had scored three tries, none of which was converted. In acute contrast Neil Jenkins had kicked five penalty goals and with time fast ticking away it was an unlikely 15 points each. Up stepped Guscott, he of the cool head and precise aim. Away the ball soared, the drop-kick perfectly executed. So it was 18-15 to the Lions. Unsung, unappreciated, notably so among a score of media people, the rank outsiders had taken the series. As they also dented several province reputations, they were splendid ambassadors, bearing comparison with the best of fellow Lions of previous years, 1974 included. What was that about those impostors, triumph and disaster?

A winning team

The HSBC Group operates through more than 5,500 offices in 79 countries and territories worldwide

HSBC Holdings plc

A WORLD OF FINANCIAL SERVICES

HongkongBank · Midland Bank · Hang Seng Bank · Marine Midland Bank · Hongkong Bank of Canada
Banco HSBC Bamerindus · Hongkong Bank Malaysia · The British Bank of the Middle East · HSBC Banco Roberts
HongkongBank of Australia · HSBC Investment Banking · HSBC Insurance

Issued by HSBC Holdings plc, 10 Lower Thames Street, London EC3R 6AE, United Kingdom

IT'S TIME YOU MADE THE CONVERSION.

When it comes to a winning team you can't beat Land Rover.

With the unmatched strength and endurance of Defender, the comfort and versatility of Discovery, the style and exuberance of Freelander and the sheer luxury of Range Rover, there's a Land Rover to suit every taste and requirement.

In addition, there's the excellent Freedom Finance package and, where status permits, Diplomatic concessions which means the best 4x4 by far is in a class of its own.

For more information call one of the numbers below and ask for Land Rover to see how they stand up to the test.

THE BEST 4x4xFAR

For details of your nearest Land Rover dealer call Freephone 0800 110 110
or write to - Land Rover, Freepost TK 494, Twickenham TW2 5UN.
Diplomatic Sales Hotline: 0181 410 8427

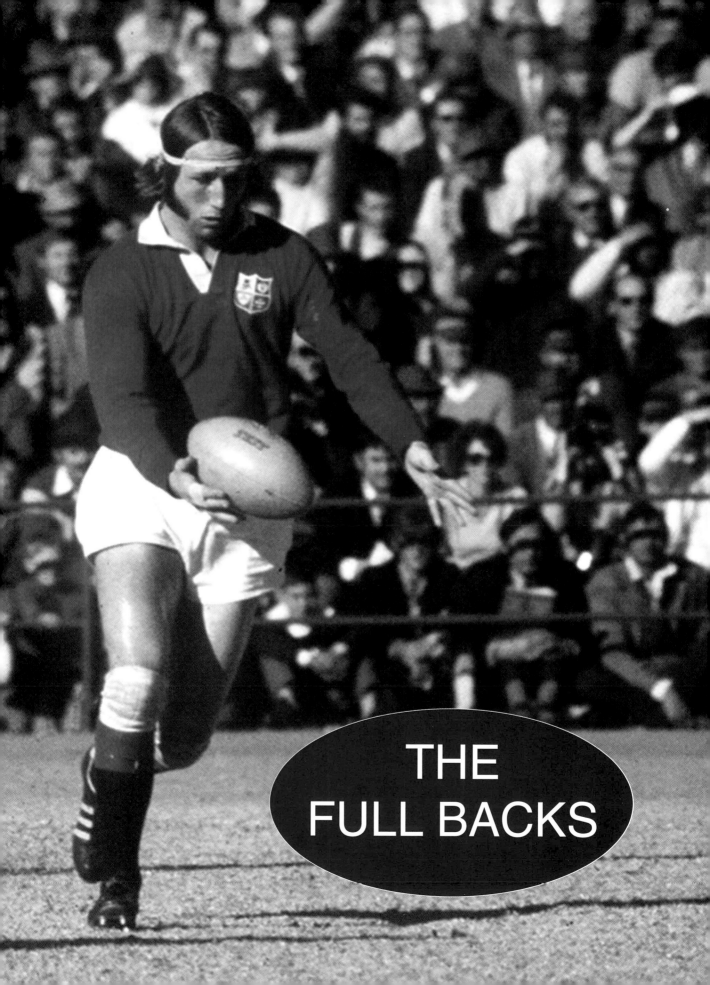

THE
FULL BACKS

J.P.R. WILLIAMS

London Welsh, Bridgend

WALES

Born 2 March 1949 , Bridgend
6ft 1in – 14st 5lbs

55 caps for Wales
first versus Scotland 1969
last versus Scotland 1981

British Lions – 2 tours, 8 Tests
1971 – New Zealand (1,2,3,4)
1974 – South Africa (1,2,3,4)

FULL BACK

John Peter Rhys Williams equalled the world record for a full back when gaining his 54th cap against Scotland at Murrayfield in February 1981 (he played once as a flanker). He thus came alongside the mark of Tom Kiernan of Ireland.

Known throughout the rugby world simply as 'JPR', he had total grasp of the orthodox full back skills, being fearless and technically sound under mortar bomb attack, as well as a bruising tackler who put his body on the line without regard for personal safety. His shoulder charge try-saving effort on Jean-François Gourdon, the French wing, at Cardiff in 1976 – it would be illegal today – saved a Welsh Grand Slam. He was a brilliant exponent of attack intrusion as, for example, at Murrayfield in 1971, he appeared like some animated genie to create the overlap for a Gerald Davies try that, along with John Taylor's touch line conversion, gave Wales a one point win that proved to be a crucial step towards another Grand Slam. He would never claim to have been a big punter but he proved a safe touch finder and was

possessed of sharp vision especially as an adventurous counter attacker.

The Welshman was a pupil at Bridgend County School and Millfield School before studying at St Mary's Hospital in London and going on to a distinguished career in medicine. At one time he was senior house officer in the University Hospital of Wales in Cardiff.

Having emerged as a player of cap potential on the Welsh tour of Argentina in 1968, JPR became a pivotal figure in a second Welsh golden era when, in the decade starting with his first cap in 1969, Wales won three Grand Slams, six Triple Crowns and eight championships, three of them shared. He played 11 times against England and never in a losing side. Of his six tries in cap internationals, five were against England and one against Ireland. He captained his country on five occasions against New Zealand in 1978 and in the 1979 championship winning side. He joined London Welsh in 1968 and proved a rare personality and on-field star in one of the most successful spells in the club's history.

A former Wimbledon junior tennis champion, JPR was the complete competitor whose calm assurance and unwavering confidence were vital ingredients in the Test successes created by the Lions in New Zealand in 1971 and in South Africa three years later. Williams was at the heart of those triumphs. In New Zealand he played in 15 of the 26 games, including the four Tests, and scored four tries. The 1971 Lions were the first to win a full series in New Zealand. Williams was a constant problem to the All Blacks at both provincial and Test level with his audacious work in attack and his ferocious tackling. He also had a key role in the 14–14 draw in the fourth Test that clinched the Lions' series win – he kicked a 45-yard drop goal to give the Lions a crucial 14–11 lead late on.

In South Africa he played in 15 of the 22 games, scored three tries and featured in all four Tests. In the final Test he made all the running for a try by Fergus Slattery that was disallowed so that the 13–13 draw robbed those Lions of a one hundred per cent record. They had to settle for played 22, won 21, drawn 1. JPR has left an indelible imprint on the rugby union game as arguably the greatest full back ever.

1974. JPR relieves the pressure against South Africa.

A.R. IRVINE

Heriot's FP

SCOTLAND

Born 16 September 1951, Edinburgh
5ft 10ins – 12st 8lbs

51 caps for Scotland
first versus New Zealand 1972
last versus Australia 1982

British Lions – 3 tours, 9 Tests
1974 – South Africa (3,4)
1977 – New Zealand (1,2,3,4)
1980 – South Africa (2,3,4)

FULL BACK

It is hard to imagine a full back scoring five tries in a representative game and especially in New Zealand – but that was the feat achieved by Andrew Robertson Irvine for the British Lions against King Country-Wanganui in 1977. One of the eight full backs to have been capped by Scotland out of the George Heriot's FP club in Edinburgh, he was arguably the most exciting and adventurous full back in the world game. Whenever he had the ball in his hands, something electric was almost bound to happen and he thrilled crowds from Edinburgh to Cape Town and Hawke's Bay with his pace and weaving running style, apart from his outstanding grasp of the game's basic skills.

At times Irvine appeared vulnerable under the high ball, not through any frailty in determination or technique but because occasionally his mind was already contemplating the next move before the ball had come into his possession. But at every level of the game he was a supreme entertainer who has become something of a legend and yet has always been admirably modest about his prodigious achievements.

Captain of George Heriot's School, he made four Scottish Schools appearances as a centre before being chosen by Edinburgh as a wing and by Scotland as a full back in his first cap international. At one time he was the most capped full back in the history of the game with 47 (he played four Scottish internationals as a wing) and also held the world record of points in internationals with 273, a tally that also included a record for a full back of 10 tries.

He captained Scotland 15 times and on three particularly memorable occasions. In December 1981 at Murrayfield he scored 17 points in Scotland's 24–15 win over the touring Wallabies; in March 1982 he led Scotland to their first win at Cardiff for 20 years, a five tries to one, 34–18 margin that was Wales's first defeat in the championship at Cardiff since 1968. Thus a run of 27 championship games at Cardiff without defeat was ended. Irvine was also captain when Scotland gained their first international win in the Southern

Hemisphere by beating Australia 12–7 in Brisbane in July 1982. That was Irvine's 50th cap.

On his three Lions' tours, Irvine played in 41 of the 66 games and in 9 of the 12 Tests. Twice in 1980 he appeared as a wing. In all he scored 274 points including 20 tries and, in 1980, a record for a Lion in South Africa of 156 points. In New Zealand in 1977 he was the top try-scorer with 11.

Andy Irvine, now a highly successful Edinburgh chartered surveyor, will always be remembered as a gifted player who had the capacity and the desire to light up the action wherever and whenever he performed.

1977. A determined run by Andy Irvine against the All Blacks.

FULL BACK

A.G. HASTINGS

Watsonians, Cambridge University, London Scottish

SCOTLAND

Born 3 January 1962, Edinburgh
6ft 2in – 14st 8lbs

61 caps for Scotland
first versus France 1986
last versus New Zealand 1995 (World Cup)

British Lions – 2 tours, 6 Tests
1989 – Australia (1,2,3)
1993 – New Zealand (1,2,3)

FULL BACK

Andrew Gavin Hastings had an exciting entry into the international arena that carried mixed fortunes. That was against France at Murrayfield in 1986. Having kicked off direct into touch, he then was faced with five Frenchmen running straight at him – they had taken a quick throw at halfway whilst everyone anticipated a scrummage at midfield. As Hastings said at the time: 'So this is what international rugby is going to be all about.' France did score but Hastings made amends: he kicked six penalty goals from all over Murrayfield to bring Scotland victory by 18–17. Thus was launched a magnificent international career which encompassed a record number of Scottish caps (until his brother Scott went four better with 65) as well as captaincy of Scotland on 20 occasions and captain of the British Lions in New Zealand in 1993.

One of four brothers, three of whom played for the Scottish Schools out of George Watson's College in Edinburgh, Gavin and his brother Scott played together in 51 cap internationals and

created another record by doing the same for the Lions in the second and third Tests in Australia in 1989.

Hastings had the ideal build for a modern full back and the high altitude bombing that proved such a large part of tactical planning. He perfected the timed jump to gather up-and-under balls and had the physique and the resolution often to stay on his feet long enough for colleagues to provide cover. He was also a master of timing, his attack intrusions at such pace as frequently to bump off defenders. This was never more true than on that famous occasion in the third and fourth place play-off in the World Cup of 1991, when he thundered into that ample and mean All Black citizen, Richard Loe of Waikato, and, to that feared man's surprise, dumped him unceremoniously backwards on to his posterior leaving Loe with the pained expression of a man unaccustomed to such treatment.

Hastings also had massive punt power and was a prolific points-gatherer. Although he has been known to miss an occasional sitter goal he

1989. Gavin Hastings, always a powerful runner, sets off with the ball against New South Wales.

holds various Scottish scoring records – most points in internationals (667), most points in an international championship season (56 in 1995), most points in an international (44 versus Ivory Coast at Rustenburg in the World Cup 1995). He was a defence pillar when Scotland won their first Grand Slam in 1990. At both Scottish and Lions' matches he oozed quiet confidence, which transmitted itself to his colleagues and was one of the most important factors behind his successful leadership of Watsonians, Edinburgh, Scotland and the Lions. In the World Cup tournaments of 1991 and 1995 he played in nine of Scotland's 10 games.

On the Lions' tour of Australia in 1989 Hastings was a mighty presence. It was his second Test try from a pass by his brother, Scott, that turned the series in favour of the Lions. In the final Test he

proved the match winner with five penalty goals and he ended the tour top scorer with 66 from two tries, one drop goal, 17 penalty goals and two conversions in seven games. The 19–12 second Test win gave the Lions the confidence to clinch the series with victory by two Tests to one. Whilst the Lions' tour to New Zealand in 1993 wasn't as successful, Hastings made a handsome impression as captain both on and off the field. He was the ideal ambassador and an inspiring leader who played in nine of the 13 games and again was top scorer, with 101 points from a try, 12 conversions and 24 penalty goals. The name of Gavin Hastings is now writ large in Scottish rugby lore as one of the best equipped full backs of all time and one who has stayed balanced in attitude and agreeably modest about his notable achievements.

FULL BACK

N.R. JENKINS

Pontypridd

WALES

Born 8 July 1971, Church Village
5ft 10in – 13st 5lbs

57 caps for Wales
first versus England 1991
still playing

British Lions – 1 tours, 3 Tests
1997 – South Africa (1,2,3)

FULL BACK

If ever you needed someone to save your life by kicking a goal from 40 yards and at an angle, the choice surely would fall upon Neil Roger Jenkins of Pontypridd, who must stand alongside that remarkable New Zealander, Grant Fox, as a goal-kicker par excellence. Time and again, Jenkins's boot has proved the difference between victory and defeat for club, country and British Lions.

Not only has Jenkins scored more points for Wales (594 in 57 games) than anyone else but he can also point to 110 points in just eight games (average 13.7 per game) during the 1997 Lions' tour in South Africa. Jenkins thus stands fourth in the all-time list of cap international scorers behind Australia's Michael Lynagh (911 in 72 games), Scotland's Gavin Hastings (667 in 61 games) and Fox (645 in 46 games). Jenkins has also proved to be such a good, all round footballer that he has represented Wales in three different positions – his 57 caps so far comprising 40 at stand off, eight at centre and nine as full back.

A Pontypridd lad who has remained loyal to his roots, Jenkins was educated at Llantwit Fardre Junior School and the Bryn Celynog Comprehensive having, as an eight-year-old, been part of the Llantwit Fardre Club scene where his father and two uncles were strong stalwarts. He played mini-rugby with Pontypridd, had his first taste of international rugby with Welsh Youth against Ireland and England in 1990 and gained his first cap as a teenager in 1991. That was against England at Cardiff on 19 January 1991, where he landed a debut penalty goal. He has been slotting them in from all over the place ever since.

He set Welsh records by scoring 24 points in each of two internationals, against Canada in 1993 and Italy in 1994. On the Welsh tour of South Africa in 1993 he set a new mark of 89 points in six games. When he took to the field against France at Cardiff on 16 March 1996 he became the most capped Welsh stand-off with 30, thus beating the record of the inimitable Cliff Morgan. Jenkins promptly celebrated with three penalty goals and a conversion in a 16–15 Welsh victory.

In the season 1993-94 he scored 451 points in 30 games for Pontypridd and Wales and he also was the first player to score a thousand points in Heineken National League history. He survived a spell in Colin Meads's King Country in New Zealand!

In the 1995 World Cup in South Africa he played in all three games for Wales, two as a centre, one at stand off, and scored 41 of their 89 points. He was voted the Welsh Player of the Year in 1994 and 1995.

When Wales won the Five Nations Championship in 1994, Jenkins scored 48 of their 78 championship points. He was in cracking form for Wales against Scotland at Murrayfield on 18 January 1997 when he scored a try, two penalty goals and four conversions for 19 points in the Welsh victory by 34–19. He could score tries all right – three against Maesteg in the sixth round of the 1996 Swalec Cup, in the final of which he landed five goals, including a drop goal, for 14 points in Pontypridd's 29–22 win over Neath.

Jenkins was undoubtedly the most influential figure in the historic 1997 Lions' Test series triumph in South Africa. He played in eight of the 13 games and as full back in all three Tests. It seemed that whenever the Lions needed a goal, Jenkins obliged with his meticulous routine that carries a touch of Fox in the way he relaxes his arms before the run-up. Jenkins scored five penalty goals in the first Test, five in the second and three penalty goals and a conversion in the third to notch up 41 of the Lions' 59 Test points. There were those who felt that he was the Lions' number one stand-off and that great benefit would have been gained by positioning him there in the Tests. Even so the ginger-haired Jenkins had a great tour and always hit the high spots when most required.

1997. The kicking of Neil Jenkins was a vital element in the decisive win against South Africa at Durban.

Whether your organisation operates in the private or the public sector in business, industry or the professions, at home or internationally – you need a law firm that understands what you need and gets results.

Dundas & Wilson is a different kind of law firm, driven by the commercial realities clients face. We recognise the importance of team management, of understanding the culture and aspirations of the client and what it takes to make a deal work. Dundas & Wilson is a member of the Andersen Worldwide international network of law firms and associated with Garretts in the Uk. As one of Scotland's largest and most progressive law firms, we bring together and develop the best people in our profession; outstanding individuals who share a vision of an organisation that is client-focused, entrepreneurial and truly international.

For more information contact
David Hardie on 0131 228 8000.

**Asking the right questions;
providing the right answers.**

At last,
a law firm that
is truly different!

DUNDAS
& WILSON

EDINBURGH   GLASGOW   LONDON

Dundas & Wilson is a member of the Andersen Worldwide international network of law firms and is associated with Garretts in the UK.

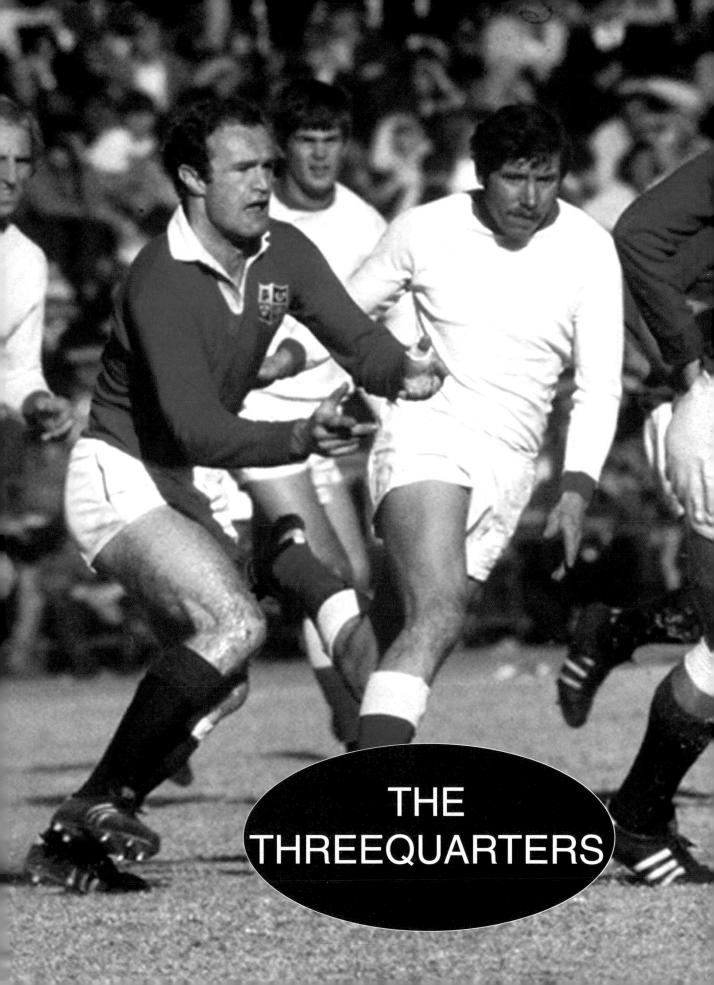

THE THREEQUARTERS

T.G.R. DAVIES

London Welsh, Cardiff

WALES

Born 7 February 1945, Llansaint
5ft 9in – 11st 8lbs

46 caps for Wales
first versus Australia 1966
last versus Australia 1978

British Lions – 2 tours, 5 Tests
1968 – South Africa (3)
1971 – New Zealand (1,2,3,4)

RIGHT WING

Thomas Gerald Reames Davies assuredly would have been one of the first names written down by anyone selecting their best World XV for, in the decade from 1967 to 1978, he was at the very heart of a halcyon spell for Wales and a Lions' tour in New Zealand that ended in their first-ever series win there. Certainly opposing wingers of his day would rate him the player they would least enjoy marking, because not only did he possess exceptional acceleratory pace, adhesive hands and an astute tactical sense, but also such gifts of running deception in jink, swerve and change of pace that likened him to an animated prairie dog and brought him an international haul of 20 tries for Wales. That tally set him alongside Gareth Edwards as his country's top try-scorer until Ieuan Evans stretched the mark to 33.

Davies was a gifted entertainer and often the spark plug to deeds of derring-do by his colleagues in the Cardiff and London Welsh clubs and on the international scene. Yet even though he was small in stature he tackled like the crack of doom and quickly embraced the modern concept of wingers acting as auxiliary full backs. Frequently, too, he worked in liaison with his Welsh and Lions' full back team mate J.P.R. Williams, to create dazzling switch moves out of defence which often left opposing defenders on the wrong foot.

Educated at Queen Elizabeth Grammar School, Carmarthen, Davies played for Welsh Schools before making a big impression in the strong Loughborough Colleges sides of the 1960s, not least in sevens where he proved a marvellous exponent. He played first for Wales as a centre against the touring Wallabies in 1966 and by 1968 had earned selection for the Lions' tour of South Africa in which, despite frustrating injury, he played in nine games including the third Test where he proved the most creative of the Lions' backs.

Blues at Cambridge University followed in 1968, 1969 and 1970 as well as the opportunity of playing in the glorious attack-minded London Welsh sides of the 1970s after he had emerged on the Welsh tour down under in 1969 as a winger of marvellous talent. He enjoyed a wonderful run in the Welsh jersey after missing 1970 through final examinations and was an influential figure in a remarkable Welsh run of three Grand Slams, five championships and five Triple Crowns. Then, in 1971, he entranced crowds all over New Zealand as a Lions' livewire in their historic Test series triumph, playing in 10 of the 26 games including all four Tests, scoring 10 tries, two of them in the second Test and a very important try early in the decisive third Test. Four of his 10 tour tries were registered in a rough match against Hawke's Bay.

He returned home with his reputation heightened and continued to impress as a wonderfully gifted wing with an elegance and style that was distinctive – the pattering steps, the light-footed surge of pace and always with a thought for his colleagues. He was the most capped Welsh threequarter with 46 until that mark was passed by Ieuan Evans against Western Samoa in June 1994. One typical Davies try was against Scotland at Murrayfield in 1971. Scotland led 18–14 with time almost up when Delme Thomas rose like a rocketing pheasant for perfectly deflected line-out ball, J.P.R. Williams intruded as extra centre and Gerald Davies scooted home for John Taylor to win the match with a soaring touch-line conversion. That was Davies par excellence, magical and sporting, one for any hall of fame.

He is now one of the most highly respected rugby journalists with *The Times*.

1971. Gerald Davies on his second Lions' tour in New Zealand.

B.H. HAY

Boroughmuir

SCOTLAND

Born 23 May 1950, Edinburgh
5ft 10in – 13st 5lbs

23 caps for Scotland
first versus New Zealand 1975
last versus New Zealand 1981

British Lions – 2 tours, 3 Tests
1977 – New Zealand
1980 – South Africa (2,3,4)

RIGHT WING

Bruce Hamilton Hay brought fame and lustre to his old school, Liberton Secondary School in Edinburgh, as their first capped player and was the Boroughmuir Club's most capped member until overtaken by his club-mate, Sean Lineen.

Hay was one of the bravest players ever to wear the thistle of Scotland. A powerfully built citizen, he was unflinching under the high ball, eminently reliable in defence with a series of bone jarring tackles and safe and long in his touch-finding. He was unfortunate to be contemporary with Andy Irvine, being a sound participant in the unsavoury chores but lacking Irvine's blinding pace and sense of adventure.

Yet Hay was a rounded enough footballer to have played five internationals at full back and 18 as a wing for Scotland, as well as having performed well in those two positions for the Lions, even though he wasn't exactly fleet of foot. Indeed when he scored the last of his three international tries against Ireland in 1981 after an interception and

50-yard dash, his colleague, Jim Renwick, always something of a wag, reckoned that it was the first time an international try had been scored live and in slow motion at one and the same time! Even so it said something for Hay's dogged approach and skills that his two other international tries were scored against New Zealand, that in 1978 being the first try for a Scottish team against the All Blacks for 43 years. Actually his first Scottish cap was in the famous waterlogged Test of 1975 in Auckland when he was preferred at full back to Irvine who played on the wing. He was unlucky to break an arm in that match but had already demonstrated that he had all the qualities to be an outstanding international player.

Hay played in five Five Nations Championships, mostly as a wing with Irvine at full back. He first played for Edinburgh in the district championship in 1972 and represented them as full back, wing and centre. That versatility, allied to his calmness under pressure, resulted in him touring New Zealand with the Lions in 1977 when he played in 11 of the 26 games and scored five tries although not selected for the Tests.

In South Africa in 1980, however, the Lions played him in the second, third and fourth Tests as a wing with Irvine, who had joined the tour party as a replacement, placed at full back. Hay made 11 appearances in all, scored the Lions' one try in the third Test and had the honour of captaining the Lions against the Country Districts and Eastern Transvaal.

A loyal and devoted Boroughmuir club man, Hay has continued his association with his club as coach and more recently as director of coaching. He will always be remembered as a great team man who never gave less than his best and who always has taken the rough with the smooth in good spirit and in good character.

1980. A strong hand-off from Bruce Hay against Northern Transvaal.

J. CARLETON

Orrell

ENGLAND

Born 24 November 1955, Orrell
5ft 10in – 12st 5lbs

26 caps for England
first versus New Zealand 1979
last versus Australia 1984

British Lions – 2 tours, 6 Tests
1980 – South Africa (1,2,4)
1983 – New Zealand (2,3,4)

RIGHT WING

That day at Murrayfield on 15 March 1980 when England wrapped up their first Grand Slam for 23 years with victory over Scotland by 30 points to 18 was a day of very special significance and memory for John Carleton. He scored three cracking tries and his performance sealed his selection for the following Lions' tour of South Africa. He had gained his first cap in 1979 when England held the All Blacks 10–9 at Twickenham having already shared in the North of England's victory over the tourists at Otley. Then to be a member of England's Grand Slam side in his first Five Nations Championship was the stuff of dreams.

He continued to serve England in the 1981, 1982, 1983 and 1984 championships and by his feats he brought fame to the Lancashire club, Orrell, who made such progress to the status of a division one club in the Courage League. He first played for Orrell as a 17-year-old and was their second capped player following prop Frank Anderson, who had played against New Zealand in 1973.

Carleton was a no nonsense type of wing. Despite having the build of a cruiserweight boxer he had genuine pace and aimed always to explode on to the ball which, when allied to his swerve, balance and aggressive hand-off, rendered him an awkward customer to put on the floor. He was a past master at checking opponents with a hint of inward thrust before easing outwards with hip sway and pace.

A former pupil of Upholland Grammar School, he qualified as a schoolmaster at Chester College, played for the England Students and British Colleges and was in the England Under 23 side in Canada and France in 1977. He proved throughout his career at every level to be a lethal finisher and one very aware of what was on offer and how to make the most of the merest chance. In that Grand Slam win over Scotland he capitalised on indecision in Scotland's back three by swooping, gathering and scoring in a thrilling 50 yard sprint.

What he might have achieved in finishing with a John Dawes, Mike Gibson or Brendan Mullin inside him will never be known but there was ample evidence to suggest that, given quality creativity inside him, Carleton might have set impressive scoring records. As it was he ran in some splendid tries for England including the three in the 1980 Grand Slam decider against Scotland, the first time for 56 years that an English back had scored a hat-trick in an international, H.P. Jacob of Oxford University and Blackheath having done so against France at Twickenham in 1924.

With the Lions in South Africa in 1980 Carleton was shamefully short of scoring chances as his mid-field colleagues found it difficult to manufacture overlap opportunities but he shone in defence chores which compensated for his running in just three tries in his 10 of the 18 tour games. He was hurt after 61 minutes of the first Test but was restored for the second Test and had the satisfaction of sharing in the Lions' 17–13 fourth Test win in Pretoria.

As a Lion in New Zealand in 1983 Carleton was concussed in the fourth match against Wellington and missed the next three games including the first Test, but he returned full of threat and vigour to top the tour try-scorers with nine, of which four were recorded in the match against West Coast at Greymouth. Unfortunately in the Tests Carleton had few chances to demonstrate that kind of finishing because the Lions' forwards couldn't emulate the mighty feats of their 1971 and 1974 predecessors. Yet Carleton played in 11 of the 18 games including three of the four Tests and ended the tour with his reputation enhanced, despite Ciaran Fitzgerald's Lions being whitewashed in the Tests.

1983. Maurice Colclough watches as John Carleton goes for the break.

I.E. EVANS

Llanelli, Bath

WALES

Born 21 March 1964, Pontardulais
5ft 10in – 13st 3lbs

72 caps for Wales
first versus France 1987
last versus Italy 1998

British Lions – 3 tours, 7 Tests
1989 – Australia (1,2,3)
1993 – New Zealand (1,2,3)
1997 – South Africa (1)

RIGHT WING

Over the years Wales has produced a shoal of jinky players who could leave opponents gasping, by sizzling off either foot in a blink. No one has sizzled to greater effect than Ieuan Cenydd Evans, the most capped Welshman of all time with 72 appearances spanning the decade 1987 to 1998. It was against Scotland at Cardiff in 1988 that he demonstrated to shattering effect those arts of deception that made him, like Gerald Davies before him, such a hard man to mark. In one of the most spectacular individualist thrusts ever seen on the famous Cardiff Arms Park pitch, he scorched inside five Scottish defenders with sidestep, swerve and pace change for a glorious try that set Wales on their way to a 25–20 win.

Evans was educated at Queen Elizabeth Grammar School, Carmarthen, and Salford University and is a member of the Gorsedd, the bardic circle at the National Eisteddfod. He joined Llanelli in 1984, was comfortably effective on either flank and, prior to joining Bath, represented them in seven cup finals.

But for five dislocations of his shoulders, a broken leg and a dislocated ankle, Evans would have had more caps but missed the entire 1989-90 international season. However, he has appeared in 11 of 12 matches in all three World Cups, has captained Wales a record 28 times, holds the Welsh record of 33 tries in cap internationals, was the first player to score 50 Heineken League tries, shares a Welsh record of four tries in a cap international (scored against Canada in the 1987 World Cup) and once roared in for six tries against Spain in 1985.

The Welshman was awarded the MBE in 1996 for services to rugby. Not only did he inspire his colleagues with his mazy running but also with his prowess in defence, which encompassed high grade anticipatory powers, sharp reactions and, when required, considerable weight of tackle.

He fitted in comfortably to the modern auxiliary full back role and to the value of considered counter attack from the deep as well as being as sharp as a tack for a scoring chance – as when, in the final Test of the Lions' tour in 1989, he followed up so speedily as to capitalise with a try when a characteristic touch of David Campese adventurism went wrong. That Evans try won the series for the Lions. Yet the Lions' back play did not quite match the success of their forwards so that not nearly enough use was made of the Evans magic. He did play in eight of the 12 games and in all three Tests but the fact that he scored only two tries reflected a failure to make the best use of his creative talents.

To some extent the same could be said of the Lions' experience in New Zealand in 1993 when their tight forwards disappointed and their very popular party lost six of 13 games. Evans however made his mark by playing in seven matches, including the three Tests which the Lions lost 2–1, as well as recording tries against North Harbour, New Zealand Maoris, Otago and Auckland, that against the Maoris in Wellington sparking off a thrilling Lions revival from 20 points down to victory by 24–20.

Evans has always possessed the magical touch that could light up a game, and his team-mates as well.

1989. Ieuan Evans at his most agile against Australia and (*below*) **1997**, on his way to one of two tries against Mpumalanga in South Africa.

RIGHT WING

S.J. DAWES

London Welsh

WALES

Born 29 June 1940, Abercarn
5ft 10in – 12st 13lbs

22 caps for Wales
first versus Ireland 1964
last versus France 1971

British Lions – 1 tour, 4 Tests
1971 – New Zealand (1,2,3,4)

Sidney John Dawes took quite a while to convince the Welsh selectors that he was worth a regular place in the national side but eventually he succeeded. He will always have a place in rugby lore as one of the finest timers of a pass the game has seen, as well as for being a tactical genius with feel and vision for what was on. He has a unique spot in rugby legend as the first player to lead a series-winning British Lions side to New Zealand and he also has a place in club legend as one who, in a sense, masterminded the advance of London Welsh to become, in the 1970s, one of the most successful and attractive club sides in the history of the game. Although first capped against Ireland in 1964 and a member of the Welsh Triple Crown side of 1965, Dawes played in only nine of the 24 Five Nations games between 1964 and 1969 before becoming established as Welsh centre in all eight championship games of 1970 and 1971. Wales shared the championship with France in 1970 and won the Grand Slam in the following year.

Having captained his country to that 1971 Grand Slam, Dawes then became the first Welsh player to captain a Lions' tour party when he linked up with Dr Doug Smith (manager) and Carwyn James (coach) in a management team that was to startle the rugby world by creating a Test series success against the All Blacks in New Zealand for the first time. It was an indication of the triumphant advance of London Welsh that Dawes had six of his club colleagues with him on that tour and that nucleus, including such greats as J.P.R. Williams, Gerald Davies, Barry John, Gareth Edwards, Mervyn Davies and John Taylor, was at the heart of the positive and adventurous attacking style that seemed straight out of London's Old Deer Park.

Those Lions time and again nonplussed the New Zealanders with the pinpoint accuracy of Barry John's kicking but also with their brilliance in constantly switching the target, as, for example, when J.P.R. Williams and Gerald Davies would work a scissors out of defence to take the attack in another direction. Behind it all was the guiding tacticianship of Dawes

CENTRE

who formed, in the four Tests, a partnership of infinite wisdom, cunning and skill with Ireland's Mike Gibson.

The touring team bore out to the letter the pre-tour forecast of their manager that they would win the Test series 2–1 with one draw. Dawes, as captain, took on the heaviest workload, playing in 19 of the 26 games and scoring five tries and a drop goal.

Having led Wales to a Slam and the Lions to a Test series win in New Zealand, Dawes seemed to have done it all. Not quite. When the 1973 touring All Blacks took on the Barbarians at Cardiff Arms Park seeking to avenge their defeat at the Lions' hands in 1971, Dawes inspired his Barbarians to a truly great performance, with London Welsh and Lions written all over it. The Barbarians won by 23–11 with a breathtaking display of audacious attack that still ranks as one of the greatest of all time. Unfortunately, having enjoyed further success as Welsh national coach between 1974 and 1979 (when they won two Grand Slams, four championships and four Triple Crowns), Dawes coached the 1977 Lions in New Zealand which proved to be an unhappy tour. It was conducted in one of New Zealand's worst winters and eventually the Lions reacted to strong and unfair criticism by the local press by cutting themselves off

1971. John Dawes and Colin Meads lead out their teams for the final Test at Eden Park, Auckland
Below
A try for the Lions' captain against Otago.

from the media. All the same, those Lions didn't lose a provincial match and the Test results were close (Lions first): 12–16; 13–9; 7–9; 9–10.

No one can deny that, during a certain period of the British game, John Dawes, London Welsh, Wales and Lions, led the way.

CENTRE

C.M.H. GIBSON

Cambridge University, NIFC

IRELAND

Born 3 December 1942, Belfast
5ft 11in – 12st 5lbs

69 caps for Ireland
first versus England 1964
last versus Australia 1979

British Lions – 5 tours, 12 Tests
1966 – Australia/New Zealand (1,2,3,4)
1968 – South Africa (1[R],2,3,4)
1971 – New Zealand (1,2,3,4)
1974 – South Africa
1977 – New Zealand

CENTRE

It surely was testimony to the versatility and manifold gifts of Cameron Michael Henderson Gibson that his record 69 caps for Ireland comprised 40 as a centre, 25 as stand-off and four as a wing. In addition to that, in his 12 Test appearances for the British Lions he was at stand-off four times and at centre on eight occasions. In the world seven-a-side tournament at Murrayfield in 1973, when the Irish surprised everyone including themselves by reaching the final, Gibson took on the role of scrum-half as to the manner born.

He was the complete all-round footballer, possessed of all the skills and of a sharp rugby brain and, whilst of slim build, he nonetheless was as tough as teak and never held back in a tackle. He once spoke of experiencing more pleasure in creating a try for a colleague than in scoring one himself and certainly he had the pace and guile and nose for space for creating overlap opportunities.

A product of Campbell College in Belfast and a Cambridge University rugby blue in 1963, 1964 and 1965, when he was captain, Gibson played first for Ireland as a stand-off in the historic 18–5 win over England at Twickenham in 1964. He represented his country in 15 Five Nations Championship matches whilst being a guiding light in their 1974 championship success. He scored 112 points for Ireland in cap internationals from 9 tries, 7 conversions, 16 penalty goals and 6 drop goals.

Like his Irish colleague, Willie John McBride, Gibson went on five Lions' tours and made such handsome contributions as to draw the highest praise from the rugby men of New Zealand and South Africa. When the Lions toured Australia and New Zealand in 1966 (he missed the Australian section because of examinations) he actually went out as a stand-off but took on the centre role in all four New Zealand Tests in order to accommodate that twinkle-toed Welshman, David Watkins, at stand-off.

With the Lions in South Africa in 1968 the Irishman also went out as stand-off and created another niche for himself by becoming the first Lions' Test

1974. Mike Gibson moves the ball down the line against Eastern Transvaal and (*below*) **1977**, once again in Lions' colours, this time against New Zealand Maoris on his fifth Lions' tour.

replacement when going on for the injured Barry John in the opening Test in Pretoria. Thereafter he played in the other three Tests as stand-off with three different scrum-half partners – Gareth Edwards, Roger Young and Gordon Connell.

Having been selected again as stand-off for the Lions' tour to New Zealand in 1971, Gibson adjusted brilliantly to the role of centre in the Tests and formed with Barry John and John Dawes a marvellously creative midfield triangle that set problem after problem for the New Zealand defenders whilst bringing the best out of the inimitable J.P.R. Williams, John Bevan, Gerald Davies and David Duckham. With Gareth Edwards at scrum half, that was a back division possessing all the arts and crafts, with Gibson supplying flair, wonderful skills, clever defence lines of running and instinctive creativity for turning a half chance into a clean incision. Having played 69 cap internationals for Ireland and 12 Tests for the Lions, Gibson, a Belfast solicitor, at one time held the record of 81 major international appearances.

A superbly disciplined and sportsmanlike player, Gibson always will be remembered as one who had it all and who always set the highest standards of effort, behaviour and attitude both on and off the field.

I.R. McGEECHAN

Headingley
SCOTLAND

Born 30 October 1946, Leeds
5ft 10in – 11st 7lbs

32 caps for Scotland
first versus New Zealand 1972
last versus France 1979

British Lions – 2 tours, 8 Tests
1974 – South Africa (1,2,3,4)
1977 – New Zealand (1,2,3[R],4)

Ian Robert McGeechan proved a somewhat undervalued Scottish midfield back, who not only was a regular choice for Scotland in seven Five Nations Championships from 1973 to 1979 but also toured twice as a player with the British Lions, playing in all eight Test matches. In addition he became a renowned coach of both Scotland and the Lions. Indeed, during the 1997 tour of South Africa McGeechan became the only one ever to coach three Lions' tours.

As a player, he was a twinkling little firefly, beautifully balanced on the run and possessed not only of fleet-footed arts of deception, notably a lightning jink off either foot, and fizzing acceleration, but with intuitive judgment of what was on and that exceptional gift of helping colleagues to play. He also had an educated left foot with which he scored seven drop goals for Scotland as well as one for the Lions in the second Test of the 1974 tour of South Africa. He was an extremely versatile player who operated 12 times as stand-off for

Scotland and 20 as centre, whilst all eight of his Lions' Tests were as a centre.

As Scotland's stand-off he fitted in with three scrum-half partners – Ian McCrae, Alan Lawson and Douglas Morgan. Although of slim build and weighing under 12 stones, he was thoroughly dependable in defence, allying clever lines of approach with unfettered commitment to copybook tackling. In approach, attitude and sporting behaviour, he was an ideal role model for younger players.

McGeechan was born in Leeds but qualified for Scotland on his father's side. He became a schoolmaster after education at Moor Grange and Allerton Grange, then Carnegie College of Physical Education. He graduated through the Yorkshire Colts to the senior Yorkshire side, after which he had his first Scottish trial in 1968. He made a drop goal cap debut against the 1972 All Blacks that cut the deficit to 10–6 before New Zealand won 14–9.

McGeechan was a good enough cricketer to play for Yorkshire Federation

CENTRE

1974. Ian McGeechan makes a break in the third Test against South Africa.

CENTRE

and Colts. Although Scotland failed to win either Grand Slam or Triple Crown during his international career, which encompassed much of Wales's second golden era, he nonetheless shared in Scotland's Murrayfield successes over the might of Wales in 1973 and 1975, and never played in a losing Murrayfield international against Ireland in four starts. He also shared in the 16–14 and 22–12 defeats of England at Murrayfield in 1974 and 1976 and played seven Tests against New Zealand, with the satisfaction of being in the Lions' side which beat the All Blacks by 13–9 at Christchurch in 1977.

Having first captained Scotland in the non-cap international against Japan in 1976 at Murrayfield McGeechan was captain in nine subsequent cap internationals. In South Africa with the 1974 Lions he was a model tourist in arguably the most successful Lions' tour, playing in 14 of the 22 games, five as

stand-off, nine as centre, including all four Tests. Those Lions won 21 games and drew the final Test 14–14. McGeechan partnered Ireland's Dick Milliken at centre in all four Tests. Apart from replacing wing J.J. Williams (Wales) in the third Test in New Zealand in 1977, McGeechan played all his other 15 games at centre and had the honour of captaining the Lions against Poverty Bay-East Coast XV and New Zealand Universities.

He has since set new marks as a Lions coach, inspiring a 2–1 Test series triumph in Australia in 1989 and another glittering Test success in South Africa in 1997. In that the Lions showed the Southern Hemisphere that they, too, could put together thrilling passages of continuous total rugby. This was much due to McGeechan's coaching. He also coached the Lions in a not quite so successful assault on New Zealand in 1993.

J.C. GUSCOTT

Bath

ENGLAND

Born 7 July 1965, Bath
6ft 1in – 13st 9lbs

52 caps for England
first versus Romania 1989
still playing

British Lions – 3 tours, 8 Tests
1989 – Australia (2,3)
1993 – New Zealand (1,2,3)
1997 – South Africa (1,2,3)

CENTRE

Few players have entered the international realm with greater impact than Jeremy Clayton Guscott who, as a 23-year-old Bath centre, strode home for three tries on his cap debut against Romania in Bucharest on 13 May 1989. He did so with that elegant, smooth acceleration, superb judgment of angle and distance, and subtle body balance in swerve and pace change, that were to decorate his career as one of the most gifted centres ever to play for England. Nor was that opening scoring performance anything of a fluke for he rattled on seven tries in his first eight cap internationals including one each against Ireland, France and Scotland in 1990, the first of his seven Five Nations Championships. In his 52 cap appearances he has scored 18 tries against 10 different countries as well as two beautifully struck drop goals against Scotland in 1992 and Wales in 1993. His 18 tries place him equal second with Cyril Lowe (Cambridge University and Blackheath) in the list of England's top try scorers. Rory Underwood is top with 49 tries.

Educated at the Ralph Allen Comprehensive School in Bath, he was a shining example of the value to clubs of a sound youth policy. He first played for Bath as a seven-year-old in their mini section and has been a loyal Bath club stalwart ever since, having represented the club in five winning cup finals. He and Will Carling created a world record 44 cap appearances as a centre partnership plus another for the Lions in the first Test against New Zealand in Christchurch in 1993. But for injuries to pelvis and groin he would have passed the 50-cap milestone earlier than 1998, for he missed England's tours to Argentina and South Africa as well as the entire 1994 Five Nations Championship. Yet he provided exceptional vision and graceful threat as a key member of England's Grand Slam sides of 1991, 1992 and 1995, their Triple Crown and championship side of 1996 and their 1998 Triple Crown side. Indeed, in his first Five Nations in 1990 he scored tries against Ireland, France and Scotland, apparently with effortless ease.

In the World Cup tournaments of 1991 and 1995 Guscott played in 10 of the 12 games and in 1992 he was honoured with inclusion in the World XV who played the All Blacks in celebration games. It was testimony to the impression Guscott created on his international debut that only a month later he was on tour with the Lions in Australia where he played in six of the 12 games. Having been overlooked for the first Test (in which the Lions were beaten 30 points to 12) he formed a potent mid-field partnership with Scott Hastings (Watsonians and Scotland) in the successful second and third Tests. He scored one of the tries of the tour in the second Test, with a deft chip ahead into space and a typical burst of pace that spurred the Lions to a 19–12 win; they clinched their first series win for 15 years with a 19–18 margin in the third Test.

Guscott was kept busy with the Lions in New Zealand, playing in nine of the 13 games including all three Tests but as the Lions tight forwards didn't always deliver the required ammunition there were fewer opportunities for the mid-field backs to put on the style. It was with some incredulity that English rugby

1997. Jeremy Guscott demonstrates his all-round contribution in the second Test against South Africa at Durban. *Left* He wraps up André Joubert and (*below*) drops the goal that won the series for the Lions.

supporters found Guscott listed as a wing against Argentina in December 1996 although he did eventually play at centre. And it hardly seems appropriate that two of his most recent caps have been as injury replacement against Ireland and Wales in the 1997 championship. With the Lions in South Africa in 1997 Guscott once again emphasised his undoubted class as one of the greats and put himself into rugby lore with the drop goal that won the second Test 18–15 and clinched the series.

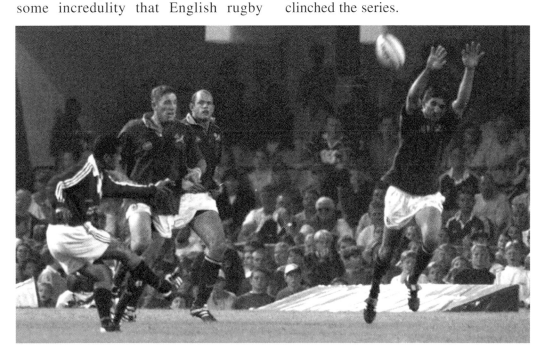

R.W.R. GRAVELL

Llanelli

WALES

Born 12 September 1951, Cydweli
5ft 11in – 13st 7lbs

23 caps for Wales
first versus France 1975
last versus Scotland 1982

British Lions – 1 tour, 4 Tests
1980 – South Africa (1[R],2,3,4)

CENTRE

That famous Welsh centre and later much respected rugby and cricket commentator, Wilfred Wooller, once described him as being 'steeped in Welshness'. Assuredly, there has been no more dedicated Welsh patriot than the bearded, piratical personality, Raymond William Robert Gravell, who breathed celtic fire and *hwyl* both on and off the field but always within the boundaries of fair sportsmanship.

Gravell was a big, raw-boned midfield man, renowned for his direct running and the impact of his tackling. He has been described as a midfield battle cruiser and he certainly took the game to the opposition with all guns blazing, a sight that time and again brought the Llanelli supporters in his beloved Stradey Park to their feet in rapturous approval.

Born in Cydweli, an ancient castle town on Carmarthen Bay, he was educated at Burry Port and at Queen Elizabeth Grammar School, Carmarthen, where the inimitable Gerald Davies had also been a pupil some six years earlier. He played for Welsh Youth and after

joining Llanelli was in the Wales B side who beat France B 35–6 at Cardiff on 21 October 1972. Ten days later, he was in the Llanelli side who beat the All Blacks by 9–3, the only Welsh side to triumph over the tourists.

Gravell's power and physical presence when allied to his unfettered enthusiasm brought him his first cap in memorable circumstances against France in Paris in 1975. He was one of six new caps in a Welsh side not highly rated but they won 25–10 and produced one of the great hack and chase tries by Pontypool's Graham Price. Gravell, the lion heart of Stradey, was well and truly launched on his cap career during which he played a notable part, especially as a crash ball specialist who set his forwards juicy targets for swift recycling and threat switches, in the Grand Slam successes of 1976 and 1978 with championships also in 1975 and 1979. He would have gained more than his 20 caps but for shoulder damage which precluded him from the entire 1977 Five Nations. On 24 January 1976

he played alongside Mike Gibson (Ireland) in the Barbarians team that beat the touring Wallabies by 19–7 at Cardiff.

It was typical of his sporting approach that when it seemed that Scottish referee Allan Hosie was about to send off Graeme Higginson, the New Zealand lock, in the Llanelli game on 21 October 1980, Gravell, then the Llanelli captain, dashed forward and pleaded for clemency. Higginson stayed on. Gravell captained Llanelli throughout that memorable season in 1980-81 when they lost only three games – to New Zealand, Leinster and the Welsh club champions, Bridgend.

As one of 15 Welshmen on the Lions tour of South Africa in 1980, Gravell played in 11 of the 18 games including the four Tests, which were lost 1–3. One report said that 'Gravell had a fine record of consistency throughout'. In the first Test he replaced the injured English wing, John Carleton, after 61 minutes and was partnered at centre in the following three Tests by Clive Woodward (England), then Paul Dodge (England). As the Lions played three different stand-offs in the Tests there was a lack of positive rhythm in the back play but Gravell always could be depended upon for total commitment to the task. That always had been his way.

1980. Ray Gravell keeps his eye on the ball during the fourth Test at Pretoria – the Lions' only win in the Test series against South Africa.

C.R. WOODWARD

Harlequins, Leicester

ENGLAND

Born 6 January 1956, Ely
5ft 11in – 12st 7lbs

21 caps for England
first versus Ireland 1980 (R)
last versus Wales 1984

British Lions – 2 tours, 2 Tests
1980 – South Africa (2,3)
1983 – New Zealand

No one can doubt that Clive Ronald Woodward of Harlequins and Leicester would have gained many more than his 21 caps but for frustrating injuries. He broke the same leg twice, once playing soccer, and shoulder damage also took its toll so that he missed one whole season. In the 1983 Five Nations Championship he played only the one game against Ireland.

Fit and on form, however, he proved to be one of the most exciting players ever to wear the rose of England, mercurial and adventurous and with those qualities of pace change and deceptive running with sizzling outward swerve that were a delight to watch but a nightmare for opposing defenders. He will always be remembered for his try against Scotland at Twickenham on 21 February 1981. It was one of the most stunning individual tries ever seen as he gained possession on a scissors with Huw Davies, came off his left foot to leave two Scots at a standstill, made a feint pass to screech inside Bill Cuthbertson, made a sizzling outward swerve to squeeze past Roy Laidlaw and

then came off his right foot to beat the cover tackle of Bruce Hay before his scoring dive. It was a key score in England's 23–17 win.

Born into a services family, Woodward was educated at HMS Conway in North Wales and at Loughborough Colleges where he came under the guiding influence of Jim Greenwood, the Scotland and Lions' loose forward, and from where Woodward graduated as a schoolmaster. He had been chosen to play for Welsh Schools against Australian Schools but couldn't because of injury. Not long afterwards he played for England Colts against Welsh Youth and for England Under 23 against Italy at Gosforth in 1976. Whilst at Harlequins he represented London against Argentina in 1978.

It provided a wonderful upsurge in his fortunes that his first cap was a prelude to his participation in all four games by which Bill Beaumont's England won, in 1980, their first Grand Slam for 23 years. When Tony Bond (Sale) suffered a broken leg in the first game of that Grand Slam against Ireland, Woodward went on

as replacement to gain his first cap and, apart from injury, never looked back. Indeed when fit he became an automatic choice, playing 15 consecutive internationals before injury struck. He scored three more tries in cap internationals – two against Argentina in Buenos Aires on 30 May 1981, two very important scores as England were held to a 19–19 draw, and one try in the 27–15 defeat of France in Paris on the 20 February 1982.

With the 1980 Lions in South Africa, a tour plagued by injuries, he played in 11 of the 18 games (only Graham Price and Clive Williams played more). He had six games as a wing and five as a centre. It was something of a surprise that Woodward was never partnered as a centre with Paul Dodge, his club colleague at Leicester, who had joined the 1980 tour as replacement and with whom Woodward had played 15 cap internationals. In the third Test both played but Woodward as wing and Dodge as centre alongside Ray Gravell (Wales). Woodward, however, made a singular contribution to the tour in emerging as a goal-kicker for 53 points (only Ollie Campbell had more, with 60) from four tries, five conversions, eight penalty goals and one drop goal. Against the South African Invitation XV at Potchefstroom, Woodward landed four

penalty goals and a conversion in the victory by 22–19, as well as being involved in one of the greatest try spectaculars – the 34 passes score – by Mike Slemen. When the Lions beat the South African Rugby Association XV at East London, Woodward contributed 16 of the 28 points. The one disappointment for the Leicester centre was when, in the third Test, and with the Lions ahead 10–6 and only 10 minutes left, he tapped a Naas Botha punt into touch. Whereupon Johannes Germishuys threw in quickly to Martinus Stofberg who returned it for Germishuys too score. Botha converted for a South African win which clinched the series for them.

Woodward had a spell in Australia when he played senior grade rugby with Manly in Sydney. In the 1983 Lions' tour to New Zealand he played in seven of the 18 games, all as centre, but did not figure in the Test series which was lost 0–4. Woodward, however, had made his mark on the game as one of its most exciting players who certainly would have revelled in the modern 'super-12' style of play.

Woodward is now the England national team coach, having been appointed at the beginning of the 1997-98 season when they gained their 20th Triple Crown.

1980.
Left Clive Woodward is pursued by Naas Botha in the second Test against South Africa and (*below*) prepares to halt an attack against Griqualand West.

CENTRE

S. HASTINGS

Watsonians

SCOTLAND

Born 4 December 1964, Edinburgh
6ft 1in – 14st 8lbs

65 caps for Scotland
first versus France 1986
last versus England 1997 (R)

British Lions – 2 tours, 2 Tests
1989 – Australia (2,3)
1993 – New Zealand

CENTRE

Only two players in the history of the rugby union game have made more cap appearances at centre than Scott Hastings, Scotland's most capped player with 65 (one as a wing). Will Carling was England's centre on 72 occasions and Philippe Sella played for France at centre 104 times plus six as a wing and once as a full back. But for injuries (hamstring at the 1987 World Cup and twice having cheek bone damage) Scott Hastings would have set a mark that, even in modern times with so many international assignments, might have stood for many years.

One of four brothers, all of whom played for George Watson's College in Edinburgh and three of whom represented Scottish Schools, Scott played 51 times in the same Scottish side as his brother, Gavin, who was Scotland's most capped player with 51 until Scott gained his 52nd against the All Blacks in Auckland on 22 June 1996.

A former captain and full back of Scottish Schools, Scott played his first game for Watsonians as a 17-year-old against Devonport Services in 1982,

captained Northumberland Under 21 and played stand-off for the Anglo-Scots whilst a student at Newcastle Polytechnic. He has played 51 games for Edinburgh, three as full back, one as wing, 47 as centre, and seven as captain. Having played for Edinburgh in three 'grand slam' district championship successes he recently captained Edinburgh in their 1996 European Cup run.

Scott's entry to the international stage was memorable when he and Gavin were two of the six new caps thrown to the French wolves at Murrayfield in 1986. The brothers' enthusiasm and confidence inspired colleagues to an unexpected 18–17 victory and was at the very heart of several Scottish successes, not least their Grand Slam triumph in 1990. Whenever Scotland's 13–7 win over England to clinch that Slam at Murrayfield is recalled, reference is bound to be made to the stunning tackle by which Scott Hastings sunk a Rory Underwood in full flight and seeming certain to score. It was a tackle that arguably saved the Slam for Scotland.

Probably the saddest spell for Scott Hastings was at the World Cup in 1987 when hamstring damage kept him out of the first two games against France and Zimbabwe and when he broke down just two minutes into the third match against Romania. He was badly missed in the quarter final when Scotland went down to New Zealand 3–30. In the World Cups of 1991 and 1995, however, he played in nine of the 10 games and, in South Africa in 1995, he scored tries against Tonga and New Zealand. A further disappointment came when he was switched to the left wing against New Zealand at Murrayfield on 20 November 1993 and his opposite number, Jeff Wilson, ran in three tries.

With the 1989 Lions in Australia he and brother Gavin created another record as the only brothers to have played together in a major British Isles Test match. Scott played in nine of the 12 games including the second and third Tests which were won 19–12 and 19–18 for a 2–1 series success. Described as 'a magnificent defensive centre with considerable presence in midfield' he formed a highly successful partnership with England's Jeremy Guscott. Not only that but his dodgy pass was scooped up by brother Gavin who then scored a crucial try in the second Test. Bad luck struck again however on the 1993 Lions' tour to New Zealand when he and Gavin were the only Scottish backs in the original selection. Having opened with a try in the 30–17 defeat of North Auckland and shared in the amazing rally from 0–20 down to 24–20 victory over the New Zealand Maoris in Wellington, he was injured in the Otago game and took no further part in the tour. Big, strong, long-striding and with a hand-off like a mule kick, with 10 cap international tries to his credit, he played three times for the Barbarians against touring sides, once as captain against the All Blacks at Cardiff on 4 December 1993.

Another highlight of his career was his captaincy of the Watsonian VII who won the prestigious Melrose tournament in 1996 for the first time for 51 years. 'A dream come true', he said. A true sportsman he has been, and a loyal team man at every grade of play.

1993. Scott Hastings tussles for possession with John Timu in the Lions' game against Otago.

I.S. GIBBS

Neath, Swansea

WALES

Born 23 January 1971, Bridgend
5ft 10in – 15st 7lbs

32 caps for Wales
first versus England 1991
still playing

British Lions – 2 tours, 5 Tests
1993 – New Zealand (2,3)
1997 – South Africa (1,2,3)

Top of the list of international centres you would least like to be pitted against would surely be Ian Scott Gibbs of Neath and Swansea. Renowned for his crash tackling, the dynamic centre has impressive pace off the mark despite his weight-lifter build.

Even at 13 stone 5 pounds in his early international matches he torpedoed opponents with shuddering impact. Since returning from rugby league, however, at a bulky 15 stone 7 pounds he has become even more formidable, not only in his physical engagement of the opponent in possession but also in his surging bursts with the ball taken at pace and in taking tackles on his terms. Certainly a major factor in the 1997 British Lions' 2–1 Test series triumph in South Africa was the number of 'big hits' made by Gibbs, irrespective of whether the target was a back or a 20-stone forward. Actually it got him into hot water when he was given a one-match suspension for punching during the 30–35 Lions' defeat by Northern Transvaal. Gibbs thus became the first Lion to be cited, although he claims that he was attempting to dislodge the ball, rugby league style.

The only player to have been in the Heineken division one championship-winning side twice running with different clubs (Neath 1991, Swansea 1992), and the son of an international gymnast, Gibbs was educated at Ysgolgyfun Llanharry, Bridgend, played for Pencoed Youth, captained Welsh Youth in 1990 and moved from Neath to Swansea in 1992.

He gained his first cap as a 19-year-old against England at Cardiff in 1991 along with another new cap, Neil Jenkins, and soon established himself as a class act by playing 18 cap internationals in a row. He missed the Zimbabwe and Namibia Tests in 1993 but returned for two tries against Japan, then switched to rugby league after playing in the 24–26 defeat by Canada in Cardiff on 10 November 1993.

He had a successful spell with Saint Helens rugby league club, winning the Championship at Wembley and the Super League in 1996 and gaining three rugby league caps for Wales.

Gibbs returned to rugby union with Swansea in the summer of 1996 and was back in the Wales side for the 31–22 win over Italy in Rome on 5 October 1996. He then played seven cap internationals in a row, became the 109th player to captain Wales when given the honour against the Americans at Cardiff in January 1997 but missed the last international of the 1997 Five Nations Championship against England because of a neck injury. On his comeback he struck up a fruitful partnership with another returnee from rugby league, Allan Bateman (Richmond). They were the Welsh centres against South Africa in 1996, and against USA, Scotland, France and New Zealand in 1997. The partnership was carried forward to the 1997 Lions' tour of South Africa when Gibbs and Bateman were midfield partners against Border, Natal and again in the second half of the third Test. They also were partners for Wales against Italy, England and Scotland in 1998.

The youngest player, at 20, ever to be judged Wales's Player of the Year, in 1991, and a try scorer in the Swansea side who beat the world champions, Australia, 21–6 on 4 November 1992, Gibbs played in six of the 13 games with the Lions in South Africa including all three Tests, in which he formed a productive midfield blend with Jeremy Guscott (England). He recovered well from injury sustained in his first appearance against Border. He played a strong part in the Lions 42–12 defeat of the powerful Natal. He had already toured with the 1993 Lions in New Zealand, playing in seven of the 13 games and gaining preference over England's Will Carling for the second and third Tests. In his very impressive tour he scored tries against Taranaki and in the third Test to add to his four tries for Wales in cap internationals against Japan in 1993 (2), the USA in 1996 and England in 1998.

Once described after his rugby league experience as 'a battle hardened warrior who enjoys confrontation with bigger men', Gibbs had played for the Barbarians against the 1992 Australians at Twickenham and the 1993 New Zealanders at Cardiff. Not surprisingly, when Wales played Western Samoa, Argentina and Australia in the 1995 World Cup, Gibbs was ever present, dynamic as always in making or taking the tackle.

1997. As ever Scott Gibbs proves difficult to bring down in the game against Natal.

D.J. DUCKHAM

Coventry

ENGLAND

Born 28 June 1946, Coventry
6ft 1in – 14st 7lbs

36 caps for England
first versus Ireland 1969
last versus Scotland 1976

British Lions – 1 tour, 3 Tests
1971 – Australia/New Zealand (2,3,4)

LEFT WING

Few English players have made a more agreeable impression on supporters than David John Duckham. Tall, blond, long-striding and adventurous, the archetypal Englishman became a firm favourite with his exciting runs during the seventies. The impact he made contrasted strangely with England's failure to gather in a Grand Slam or Triple Crown during his international career between 1969 and 1976.

Duckham allied his physical presence as a big man with genuine pace to the subtle arts of deception and superb balance at speed. He was a prolific try scorer. During two and a half seasons between 1968 and 1970 he ran in 70 tries, he holds the British Lions' record of six tries in one game against West Coast-Buller in New Zealand in 1971, and he recorded five tries in a match for the Barbarians against Leicester and also for Coventry against Fylde, both in 1969.

A former pupil of the King Henry VIII School in Coventry, he played old boys' rugby before joining Coventry as a 21-year-old in 1968. Such was the impression he made that he was capped

a few months later. It was no great surprise that he scored a try on his debut against Ireland in Dublin on 8 February 1969 by suddenly materialising at pace outside Rodney Webb, his Coventry team-mate, and making a thrilling dash to the corner. That was the first of his 10 cap international tries that included four against France, two of them in the 14–6 Twickenham win over the French on 24 February 1973. Duckham had the distinction of scoring tries against each of the Five Nations Championship countries.

Whenever Duckham had the ball in his hand there was an air of expectancy among the spectators because he enjoyed tilting his lance and was a thrilling sight when he stepped on the gas. He held the English record for a back of 36 caps and formed a potent centre partnership with John Spencer (Cambridge University and Headingley) in 10 cap internationals. Indeed there was strong criticism of the English selectors for Duckham being switched to the wing for 22 games although he enhanced his reputation as a wing for the Barbarians and notably with the 1971 Lions in Australia and New Zealand. On that tour he played in 16 of the 26 games and gained preference over Cardiff's John Bevan for the second, third and fourth Tests as the Lions won a full Test series in New Zealand for the very first time. Duckham was also second top try scorer on tour with 11. He was ideally suited to the fluent style embraced by those Lions and to the flamboyant counter attack switches involving full back J.P.R. Williams (Wales) and his wings. In the final Test in Auckland, when the Lions gained a 14–14 draw to clinch their series win, Duckham gave a memorable tackling display. In his book about the tour, John Reason wrote that Gerald Davies showed true world class, while 'David Duckham was not far behind which was a remarkable achievement considering that he much prefers to play at centre'.

One of Duckham's greatest displays was for the Barbarians in their 23–11 defeat of the All Blacks at Cardiff on 27 January 1973, when he demonstrated all of his attack talents to thrilling effect. He had already represented the Barbarians as a try scorer against the 1971 South Africans and later played for them against the 1974 New Zealanders. He also had the satisfaction of sharing in England's 16–10 defeat of New Zealand in Auckland on 15 September 1973.

Yet he stayed loyal to his roots as a Coventry stalwart and captain who was promoted to the Warwickshire side after only eight senior club games and who captained the West Midlands to their 16–8 win over the touring All Blacks at Birmingham on the 6 December 1972. It was a pity only that Duckham did not have a world cup competition in which to show his style to the world audience. They would have been duly impressed.

1973
David Duckham takes on the All Blacks again, this time in Barbarian colours.

J.J. WILLIAMS

Bridgend, Llanelli

WALES

Born 1 April 1948, Nantyfllyllon
5ft 9in – 12st

30 caps for Wales
first versus France 1973 (R)
last versus England 1979

British Lions – 2 tours, 7 Tests
1974 – South Africa (1,2,3,4)
1977 – New Zealand (1,2,3)

LEFT WING

Over the years Wales has produced a galaxy of 'quickies' who could burn the grass to sizzling effect: perhaps the quickest of all has been John James Williams, known to all as 'JJ', who was Welsh sprint champion and competed in the 1970 Commonwealth Games. A slimly built fellow, he didn't exactly exude physical dimension or power and would have been out of place as a crash-ball type but he compensated with flaring acceleration, the gift of pace change to order, a keen anticipatory sense and became master of the little kick ahead and chase, all of which brought him a barrow-load of tries.

He proved an all round sports type in his early days having represented the Welsh Secondary Schools at rugby and athletics out of Maesteg Grammar School and having opted for rugby with Bridgend before switching to Llanelli and sharing in some of the great triumphs at Stradey Park. He became a schoolmaster after graduating from Cardiff College of Education but when he was unable to obtain leave of absence

for the 1974 Lions' tour of South Africa, he went into marketing and so had no similar problems in 1977 about touring with the Lions in New Zealand.

Williams gained his first cap as replacement for Arthur Lewis (Ebbw Vale) in the 3–12 defeat by France in Paris on 24 March 1973 and so launched a cap career of high success, not least in his immediate acceptance by the Welsh selectors as a regular. All 30 of his caps were consecutive and as Wales had Gerald Davies on the other wing (J.J. Williams switched from right to left wing to accommodate Davies), Wales were blessed with exceptional pace and skill on each wing during their second golden era of the seventies.

Once, when Gerald Davies was injured JJ moved to the right wing against John Hipwell's touring Wallabies on 20 December 1975 and promptly scored three of his 12 cap international tries in a Welsh win by 28 points to 3. His third try, not surprisingly, was from his own chip ahead, pinpoint in its accuracy and bringing to mind a try he had scored in the 16–16 draw with France in 1974 when he kicked ahead then actually kneed the ball high over the French line, caught it on the follow-up and scored. When Llanelli held those Australians to a 28–28 draw, Williams again was a try scorer.

He scored tries against the other four countries in the Five Nations and in 1975-76 he rattled up a tally of nine tries in seven games – against Japan (two tries twice) in Osaka and Tokyo, three against Australia and one each against Scotland and France in the 1976 championship.

During two Lions' tours Williams equalled and created records and gained the respect of New Zealanders and South Africans alike with his sizzle and try-scoring acumen. In 1974, after just one season of international rugby, he went with the Lions to South Africa, played in 12 of the 22 games including all four Tests, scored 12 tries and set a new mark

match in the third Test, following his two brilliant tries, he was described as 'having produced memorable moments to delight South African crowds'.

The 1977 Lions in New Zealand were not quite as successful, but J.J.Williams played in 14 of the 25 games including the first three Tests, missing the fourth because of hamstring damage. He scored 10 tries including one in the 13–9 Test win in Christchurch when he dummied, hinted at the inside break but instead veered outwards for a brilliant score. Thus on two Lions' tours he played in 26 games and was in the losing side only twice and that in Test matches. Considering that he also shared in that remarkable spell when Wales won three Slams, four championships and four Triple Crowns between 1974 and 1979, truly it could be said that J.J. Williams enjoyed heady success in the very top echelons of the game.

1974.
J.J. Williams goes over for one of his two tries against South Africa in the third Test.

with four Test tries. The Lions created an unbeaten record over the 22 games (there was one draw) and won the Test series 3–0. The Welshman also equalled David Duckham's 1971 record by scoring six tries against the South West Districts at Mossel Bay. Declared the man of the

G.R.T. BAIRD

Kelso

SCOTLAND

Born 12 April 1960, Kelso
5ft 9in – 12st

27 caps for Scotland
first versus Australia 1981
last versus Ireland 1988

British Lions – 1 tour, 4 Tests
1983 – New Zealand (1,2,3,4)

LEFT WING

Kelso Rugby Club in the Scottish Borders has earned fame, among other things, for spawning six outstanding international loose forwards – Jimmy Graham, Ken Smith, Charlie Stewart, Eric Paxton, John Jeffrey and Adam Roxburgh – but the club also produced one of the most gifted international threequarters in Gavin Roger Todd Baird who was an automatic choice as Scotland's wing during the eighties. Not only was Baird a beautifully balanced, long-striding runner with startling pace (that enabled him once to win three sprint titles at the one Border Athletics championship meeting) but he was a good all-round footballer with soft hands and an agile rugby brain. There was a touch of the Rolls Royce about him when in full flow.

He played scrum half for Scottish Schools against Ireland and England in 1978, having been educated at St Mary's School in Melrose and at Merchiston Castle School in Edinburgh. His club, however, switched him to the wing in their eminently successful seven-a-side squad and it was as a wing that he played

in 26 cap internationals with one appearance also as a centre against England at Twickenham on 4 April 1987.

Having toured with Scotland in New Zealand as a 20-year-old in 1981, Baird enjoyed a thrilling baptism to cap status in the 24–15 win over the 1981 touring Australians at Murrayfield. His fifth international appearance was in an historic Scottish win at Cardiff in 1982, the margin 34–18, the first home defeat of Wales in the Five Nations Championship for some 24 years. It was in that Cardiff victory that Baird underlined his gifts as a counter attacker when he gathered a Gareth Davies punt near his own line and surged up the left touch line to set up a wonderful try by Jim Calder (Stewart's-Melville FP).

Baird has had his leg pulled about the fact that in 27 cap internationals for Scotland he never scored a try. Indeed his only international try was for the 1983 British Lions in New Zealand. There was a Baird try against Romania in Bucharest in 1986 but it was disallowed for a dubious foot in touch. Nonetheless Baird was a lethal runner-in who scored a record 29 tries in 21 games for the South of Scotland for whom he first played in 1979. He also was in the South side who beat the 1984 Grand Slam Australians by 9–6 at Hawick, a fixture in which his father, Roger, a powerful, crash-tackling Watsonians and Edinburgh centre, had played in 1957. Roger junior often played inside centre for his club, Kelso, being a member of their side who won the Scottish national league championship in 1988. The South, Scotland and the Lions, however, all played him as a wing.

Among other highlights in the Baird career was membership of the Scottish side who recorded their first ever win down under when they beat Australia by 12–7 in Brisbane on 4 July 1982 and he played a full part in Scotland's 1984 Grand Slam, 59 years after their first in 1925. In the England match of 1986 Baird again turned defence into thrilling attack when he swooped on a wayward English pass and exploded off his mark to ignite a sweeping move ending in a try for Scott Hastings.

Baird was in Scotland's squad at the World Cup down under in 1987 but was one of four who did not get a game. On Scotland's tours of New Zealand and Australia in 1981 and 1982, however, he had played in 10 of the 17 tour games. He had an equally demanding workload with the 1983 Lions in New Zealand, when he played in 11 of the 18 games including those against Auckland, Wellington, Manawatu, Wairarapa-Bush, Canterbury, Counties and Waikato as well as the four Tests. He was second top try scorer with six, one of which was in the third Test in Dunedin when he chased a kick ahead, showed admirable foot control in dreadful conditions and splashed over. So he shared with his countryman, John Rutherford, the honour of scoring the only Test tries for the Lions. Baird was also instrumental in turning impending defeat into victory against Wellington who had led 13–6: however, the Scotsman scored two tries and made another for Michael Kiernan (Ireland) to inspire a Lions' triumph by 27–19.

Baird was described in one tour assessment as being 'one of the few to gain credit from a disastrous tour'. Roger the Rolls had made it at the top.

1983. Roger Baird breaks through the All Black defence in the second Test at Wellington.

R. UNDERWOOD

Leicester, RAF

ENGLAND

Born 19 June 1963, Middlesbrough
5ft 9in – 14st

85 caps for England
first versus Ireland 1984
last versus Ireland 1996

British Lions – 2 tours, 6 Tests
1989 – Australia (1,2,3)
1993 – New Zealand (1,2,3)

LEFT WING

Of all the great strike runners spawned by the rugby union game, Rory Underwood's name would be high on the list, for England have never had a more lethal finisher or scorer of spectacular tries. The reasons for this were his explosive pace off the mark, his exceptional balance in subtle changes of direction, his static strength and stocky frame at some 14 stones, his instinctive feel for support positioning and, to some extent also, the fact that he played in the wake of some formidable ball winning forwards and with gifted colleagues inside him such as Simon Halliday, Kevin Simms, Will Carling and Jeremy Guscott.

Underwood could play effectively on right or left wing and, whilst he was not quite as dependable going backwards as forwards, providing some scary moments in retreat defence and with no great pretensions to being a punt expert, he yet was a successful policeman of opposing quickies and one capable of making his audience gasp in astonishment whether in advance or retreat.

A former pupil of Barnard Castle School in Durham (where Rob Andrew was a contemporary) he graduated through England Colts, Under 23 and B team levels before starting on a 13-season reign as international wing. He has the remarkable record of having played in 50 of 51 Five Nations Championship games throughout his career, having missed only the Scotland international of 1986. He is now the most capped wing in the history of the game, with 85 appearances for England as well as six Tests for the British Lions – David Campese has 101 caps but 16 were as a full back. Underwood lies second in the list of cap international try scorers with 49 tries against 12 countries, Campese having registered 64.

With five tries against Fiji in 1989 Underwood equalled the then world record, since eclipsed by the New Zealander Marc Ellis with six against Japan in the 1995 World Cup. Against Scotland at Murrayfield in 1991 Underwood became the first England player to reach the 50 caps milestone.

On England's tour to Australia and Fiji in 1988 he scored six tries in four games and in four internationals in 1989-90 he achieved nine tries. He was England's Grand Slam wing in 1991, 1992 and 1995 with seven tries and he played in all three World Cups with appearances in 15 of the 16 games. He would have amassed more caps but for his RAF duties as a jet pilot which prevented him from touring with England in South Africa in 1984, New Zealand in 1985 and Argentina in 1990.

Underwood was a member of the triumphant Lions' tour to Australia in 1989 playing in eight of the 12 games including all three Tests. He kept very close tabs on the nippy Australian wing, Ian Williams. He scored two tries against West Australia and two against New South Wales B at Dubbo which brought the crowd to its feet as he scorched his way through cluttered confines for thrilling scores.

With the Lions in New Zealand in 1993 he played in seven of the 13 games, including all three Tests. He scored tries against North Auckland and New Zealand Maoris as well as a touch-line dash try that stretched the Lions' lead to 17–7 in the second Test which they eventually won 20–7. On that tour he was a rival with his younger brother Tony for the left wing berth. Against South Africa at Twickenham in 1992 they had become the first brothers to play together in an England cap international since the Wheatleys, Arthur and Harold, against Scotland in 1937.

1993. Rory Underwood on the burst against New Zealand in the third Test at Eden Park, Auckland.

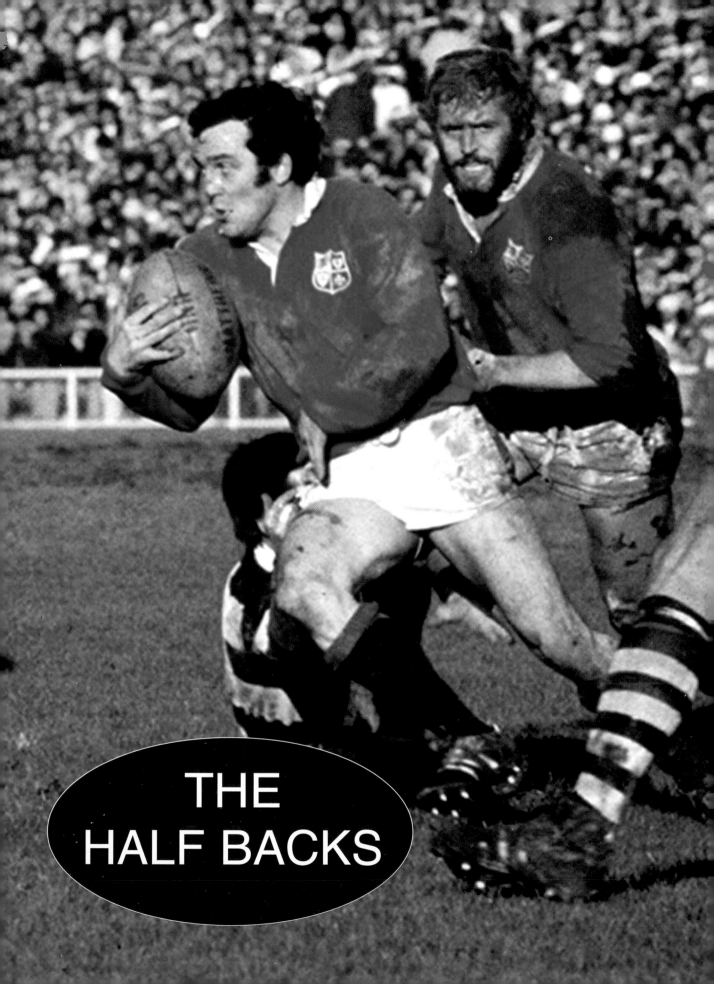

THE
HALF BACKS

B. JOHN

Llanelli, Cardiff

WALES

Born 6 January 1945, Cefneithin
5ft 9in – 11st 11lbs

25 caps for Wales
first versus Australia 1966
last versus France 1972

British Lions – 2 tours, 5 Tests
1968 – South Africa (1)
1971 – New Zealand (1,2,3,4)

He flitted like some phantom through the cluttered confines of the opposing defences, like some waif possessed of hypnotic powers and skill – that surely is an apt description of the subtle modes of deception and wizardry that made Barry John such an extraordinary talent, not to mention his mastery of flight and distance in the placement of his punts. Like all the truly great participants, he always seemed able to manufacture time and space for himself. He also possessed superb control of sidestep, dummy and change of pace, all of which proved mystifying to his opponents who tended to be taken in by his slim build.

John learned a great deal about the special requirement of the stand-off role from, as a youngster, watching Carwyn James practising in their home village of Cefneithin, as well as from playing for Llanelli. By coincidence it was the coaching brilliance of James that brought out the playing and tactical brilliance of John which undoubtedly underpinned the great Lions' triumph in 1971, the first time they had won a Test series in New Zealand.

A former student of Gwendraeth Grammar School and Trinity College, Carmarthen, John later became a prolific points scorer in representative games, at one time holding the Welsh record of eight drop goals in internationals. He beat Jack Bancroft's record of 88 points in Welsh cap internationals with 90, from five tries, eight drop goals, 13 penalty goals and six conversions. In the 1972 championship, curtailed as it was by the internal troubles in Ireland, he scored 35 of Wales's 67 points for another Welsh championship record – and that in just three games.

He developed his goal kicking with a simple round the corner, right foot style, never appearing to whack the ball but rather to coax it over in a friendly manner. Yet he landed some big goals. When Wales won their 1971 Grand Slam he contributed 31 of their 73 points and he showed admirable bravery in scoring a crucial try in the final game against France in Paris despite having suffered a damaged nose in tackling, head on, the mighty French forward, Benoit Dauga.

FLY HALF

John and Gareth Edwards were the Welsh halves in 23 cap internationals. Edwards once described the pleasure of taking a salmon on one of his angling sorties thus: 'It was fully 17 pounds', he said, 'almost as big as Barry John'. They played together in three Welsh championship sides, the Triple Crown team of 1969 and that great Slam side of 1971 that formed the broad nucleus of the 1971 Lions' triumph in New Zealand.

John had already toured in South Africa in 1968 but following appearances against Western Province, South West Districts and Natal, he suffered a broken collarbone in the opening Test in Pretoria after just 15 minutes play and took no further part in the tour. It was a different story in Australia and New Zealand three years later. John so dominated the proceedings with tactical and technical brilliance as to be referred to by all as 'the King'. He also set a tour record of 191 points in 17 games from 7 tries, 31 conversions, 28 penalty goals and 8 drop goals. In the four Tests he contributed 30 of the Lions' 48 points. No wonder even the hard-boiled New Zealand press agreed that he was a master of his rugby union trade.

1971. Barry John, the 'King' of Wales and the mastermind behind the Lions' historic series win in New Zealand.

P. BENNETT

Llanelli

WALES

Born 24 October 1948, Felin-Foel
5ft 7in – 11st

29 caps for Wales
first versus France 1969 (R)
last versus France 1978

British Lions – 2 tours, 8 Tests
1974 – South Africa (1,2,3,4)
1977 – New Zealand (1,2,3,4)

FLY HALF

It was that twinkle-toed stutter prior to coming off either foot in a blink or simply stepping on his accelerator like a sprinter off his block that helped to make Phil Bennett a special type of player who took such a creative role in some of the most spectacular tries ever seen.

There was that Gareth Edwards try for the Barbarians against the 1973 All Blacks that all started with Bennett magically turning desperate defence into scintillating attack with an assortment of sizzling sidesteps that left his opponents cross-eyed. There was another dazzling effort over 50 yards for his try in the second Lions' Test against South Africa in Pretoria in 1974. He also exploded off his right foot in a blur and at full tilt to score between Scotland's posts at Murrayfield in 1977 as the climax to another breathtaking attack out of a panic area, with J.P.R. Williams providing the torch.

At the end of his international career Bennett held the Welsh points scoring record with 166 in 29 games from 4 tries, 18 conversions, 2 drop goals and 36 penalty goals. It was no easy task, of course, to follow in the footsteps of the inimitable Barry John and, although Bennett had represented Wales at school and youth levels, it was some time before he established himself in the stand-off role. He became the first Welsh player to go on as a substitute when Gerald Davies injured his elbow against France at Colombes Stadium in 1969, but Bennett was on at centre for only four minutes and didn't touch the ball.

In 1970 he took on the role of utility player. He was at centre against Scotland, wing against South Africa and stand-off against France. In 1972 against Scotland he went on at full back to replace the injured J.P.R. Williams.

He played his first full Five Nations in 1973 as stand-off after having shared in that pivotal position in the famous Barbarians' triumph against Ian Kirkpatrick's 1972-73 All Blacks. With the Lions in South Africa in 1974 Bennett flourished behind a magnificent pack: he played in 11 of the 22 games including all four Tests, scored 103 points that included 26 in Tests, and was a central figure in the Lions' Test series triumph of three wins and one draw.

In 1977 he experienced the high honour of captaincy of the Lions in New Zealand but that tour was blighted by dreadful weather and inconsistent management. Little rapport was established with the media. Yet the Lions lost only one game outside the Test series – to New Zealand Universities – and, although Bennett did not reach his personal heights of the 1974 tour in South Africa, he did play in 14 of the 26 games and was top scorer with 125. Amongst these, 18 were notched up in the New Zealand Tests and 13 in the closing match against Fiji in Suva.

It was towards the end of his international career that Bennett enjoyed further fulfilment. He captained Wales in all eight games of the 1977 and 1978 Five Nations Championships, achieving the championship and Triple Crown in 1977 and a Grand Slam in 1978.

There were times when 'Benny' fell below his vast potential but his adhesive hands, his educated boot, his nose for space and those shimmering sidesteps have earned him a merited place in Wales's hall of fame. He could light up a game with pure genius.

1977. After successfully taking over the mantle of Barry John in South Africa in 1974, Phil Bennett took on the captaincy of the Lions for their next trip to New Zealand.

S.O. CAMPBELL

Old Belvedere

IRELAND

Born 5 March 1954, Dublin
5ft 10in – 12st

22 caps for Ireland
first versus Australia 1976
last versus Wales 1984

British Lions – 2 tours, 7 Tests
1980 – South Africa (2[R],3,4)
1983 – New Zealand (1,2,3,4)

FLY HALF

High on the list of Northern Hemisphere players to match the goal-kicking feats of Grant Fox of New Zealand surely would be that favourite son of Anglesey Road in Dublin, Seamus Oliver Campbell, known to his friends as 'Ollie'. His ability to steer the ball between the posts from all angles made him a key figure in Irish international rugby during the eighties and notably in their Triple Crown and championship successes of 1982 and 1988.

Supporters of the Old Belvedere club have spoken of those evenings, when, following squad practice, they would be enjoying their refreshments to the distant thump of boot on ball, in darkness relieved only by training light. That was the young Campbell, creating the confidence, technique and timing that were to make him one of the most prolific scorers in Irish rugby and one who, in some internationals, scored all of their points. No more convincing demonstration of this was given than in the 1982 Triple Crown decider with Scotland in Dublin. John Rutherford scored the only try of the game for the

Scots but Campbell clinched the crown for Ireland with an extraordinary display of goal-kicking for six penalty goals and one drop goal, thus scoring all 21 points in Ireland's 21–12 victory. It was a testing, blustery day, the pitch dampish, evil conditions for a goal-kicker, but, as if guided by radar, Campbell slammed over goal after goal from all over the pitch to set a then Irish record for one international, an achievement he equalled a year later against England in Dublin. He still holds the Irish record for most points scored in a Five Nations Championship – 52 in 1983 – whilst he shares, with the legendary Dickie Lloyd, the Irish record of seven drop goals in internationals. His 217 points in 22 cap internationals was also an Irish record until beaten by Michael Kiernan with 308 points in 43 internationals between 1982 and 1991.

Educated at Belvedere College and the College of Commerce in Dublin, Campbell missed 16 internationals after his first cap against Australia in 1976 before finding favour again. He made a strong impression on the Irish tour of

Australia in 1989 when he set a record of 60 points in five games including 28 of Ireland's 36 points in winning the two Tests. In the 1980 Five Nations Championship he scored a then record 46 points. He contributed another 46 of Ireland's 66 points in winning the

championship and Triple Crown in 1982 and a year later, when Ireland shared the championship with France, his share was 52 of Ireland's 71 points.

Although renowned as a tactical kicker from place and hand he proved also to be a perceptive runner with ball in hand, quick and with an eye for space and, for one of such slim contours, an intuitive cover defender and tackler.

With the Lions in South Africa in 1980 he suffered hamstring damage, playing in only seven of the 18 games including the three Tests, yet was top scorer with 60 points. In New Zealand with the Lions in 1983 he gave some impressive performances in provincial games and finished top scorer with 124 points from 11 appearances. In the Tests, however, he was short of quality ball and unable to prove the catalyst to the Lions' back division. Ireland has had reason to be grateful for Campbell's team spirit, loyalty, unfettered commitment and exceptional goal-kicking.

1980
Below Ollie Campbell gets the line moving against South Africa and (*left*) **1983**, in possession against Waikato.

C.R. ANDREW

Cambridge University, Nottingham, Wasps, Toulouse, Newcastle

ENGLAND

Born 18 February 1963, Richmond
5ft 9in – 11st 4lbs

71 caps for England
first versus Romania 1985
last versus Wales 1997

British Lions – 2 tours, 5 Tests
1989 – Australia (2,3)
1993 – New Zealand (1,2,3)

FLY HALF

It was somewhat unusual for a 21-year-old to drop a goal within 50 seconds of the start of his debut international, then complete the match with a haul of 18 points – but that is how Christopher Robert Andrew launched a cap career that had a few lows but a great many highs. He remains the most capped stand-off in the history of the game, with 70, plus another cap as a full back against Fiji in Suva in June 1988.

That remarkable debut performance was in the 22–15 win over Romania at Twickenham in January 1985 and it is just one of several astonishing scoring feats by Andrew. For instance: his six penalty goals and one drop goal in the 21–18 defeat of Wales at Twickenham in 1986, his five penalty goals and one drop goal in the 18–14 victory over France in Paris in 1994, his 27 points in the 32–15 triumph over South Africa in Pretoria in June 1994, his 54 points in two consecutive internationals against Romania and Canada in 1994 and all 24 points in the 24–18 defeat of Argentina in the 1995 World Cup in South Africa. He

holds the English record of 396 points in cap internationals, the world record of 21 drop goals for England plus two for the Lions, and at one time he held the record of 30 points in one international, against Canada at Twickenham in 1994. Remember, too, his sensational match-winning drop goal against Australia in the quarter final of the World Cup in 1995?

Andrew was educated at Barnard Castle School in Durham and was a Cambridge University Blue in 1982, 1983 and 1984, amassing 36 points from his three Varsity games. He captained Cambridge University at cricket, played rugby for Durham Schools 19 Group, Yorkshire, Northern Division and five fine clubs, Nottingham, Wasps, Toulouse, Gordon in Sydney, Australia, and Newcastle.

Andrew was thoroughly well equipped, technically and tactically, with a cricketer's hands, punt control off either foot, a willing and jarring tackler and with the discipline to hold to the team strategy even though there were times when this was not over popular with the English support. During his international reign from 1985 to 1997 England played much percentage rugby, with its foundation in Andrew's inch-perfect punt placements which gave a lot of ball to their big heavy forwards. Sometimes it wasn't pretty to watch but Andrew dictated the trend in commanding fashion and it was in large measure through his direction and control that in 1991, 1992 and 1995 England gathered in three Grand Slams.

It seemed in every sense appropriate that, having apparently gained his last cap against France in the 1995 World Cup, he was called back to the colours to replace the injured Mike Catt after 72 minutes of the match against Wales in 1997. England won by 34–13 and so Andrew was involved, even if only briefly, in his country's 20th Triple Crown success.

Not an original choice for the Lions' tour of Australia in 1989, Andrew joined the party as replacement for the Irishman Paul Dean (cartilage damage) and his control and positive attitude as well as his partnership with Welsh scrum half Robert Jones had much to do with the Lions winning the second and third Tests and thus the series by 2–1. Andrew thus became the first English stand-off for 27 years to play for the Lions in a Test, the last having been Richard Sharp against South Africa in 1962.

Andrew played in all three Tests in New Zealand in 1993 for the Lions, his partner being his English colleague, Dewi Morris, and he had a big influence on the 28–10 defeat of Canterbury with a try, a conversion, a penalty goal and a drop goal. He also slotted an important drop goal in the 20–7 win in the second Test.

Undoubtedly one of the great points-scorers, Andrew was a better all-round footballer than he was given credit for, and a marvellous goal-kicker with his characteristic jack-knife and crouched run up leading to some superb goals, even when the pressure was intense.

1989. Rob Andrew played a major role in winning the series in Australia after the Lions had lost the first Test.

G.O. EDWARDS

Cardiff

WALES

Born 12 July 1947, Pontardawe
5ft 8in – 13st 5lbs

53 caps for Wales
first versus France 1967
last versus France 1978

British Lions – 3 tours, 10 Tests
1968 – South Africa (1,2)
1971 – New Zealand (1,2,3,4)
1974 – South Africa (1,2,3,4)

SCRUM HALF

It was a clear indication not only of Gareth Owen Edwards's durability but of his exceptional consistency in top form that he played in 53 cap internationals in a row for Wales, never once was dropped and only once was replaced because of injury. (That was against England at Twickenham in 1970 when Ray 'Chico' Hopkins gained his one cap.)

Edwards had a central role in a second Welsh 'golden era' in that he played in 12 consecutive Five Nations Championships during which Wales won three Grand Slams, five Triple Crowns and seven championships (two shared).

He was immensely strong, especially in the upper body, possessing the barrel-chest of a shot putter as well as powerful legs, arms and wrists. In addition, he exhibited a strong competitive instinct and a willingness to acknowledge his vulnerable areas (there weren't many of them) and to work on them until he reached the standard he knew was essential for survival in the highest echelon. Not initially a particularly shrewd tactician, he developed a feel for

what was required. He also improved the pace and length of his service and worked on perfecting a repertoire of punts that created all kinds of headaches for opposing defenders. From short range, ball in hand, he was almost unstoppable. His games teacher and mentor at Pontardawe Grammar Technical School, Bill Samuel, made sure that Edwards not only concentrated on the scrum half role but also developed gymnastic and athletic ability that was to rate him in the eyes of many as the greatest scrum half of all time. Exceptional fitness also was an Edwards hallmark as demonstrated in two special tries that he scored – when he exploded from nowhere for the try of all tries for the Barbarians against the 1972 All Blacks at Cardiff, and also when he scored a long range chip ahead try against Scotland at Cardiff in 1972.

Edwards attended Pontardawe Technical School before representing Welsh Secondary Schools out of Millfield School, then became a Cardiff College of Education graduate before being capped as a 19-year-old against France in 1967.

1971. Gareth Edwards in New Zealand and (*below*) **1974**, in South Africa – a giant in two legendary teams.

He became the youngest player ever to captain Wales when, aged 20 years and seven months, he took on that role against Scotland in only his fifth international. At one time he held jointly with Gerald Davies the Welsh record of 20 cap international tries until that mark was passed by Ieuan Evans against Romania in 1994. Gareth Edwards was the first Welshman to reach the milestone of 50 caps. His partnership with Barry John is now indelibly printed in legend. The 'ham and eggs' of Welsh rugby was how they once were described and their influence on Welsh success with the Lions was massive for each exuded a quiet confidence, each was very much part of the other. They first played together for Wales against the mighty 1967 All Blacks and were partners in 23 internationals, including the Grand Slam sequence of 1971.

Having suffered shoulder damage, Edwards missed the third and fourth Tests with the Lions in South Africa in 1968 but firstly in partnership with Barry John, then with Phil Bennett, he was a central figure in the Lions' historic Test series triumphs in New Zealand 1971 and South Africa 1974. Edwards played scrum half in all eight of those Tests and even the stern men of New Zealand and South African rugby had to admit that he was something else.

R.N. JONES

Swansea

WALES

Born 10 November 1965, Trebanos
5ft 7in – 11st 5lbs

54 caps for Wales
first versus England 1986
last versus Ireland 1985 (World Cup)

British Lions – 1 tour, 3 Tests
1989 – Australia (1,2,3)

SCRUM HALF

Wales have never been short of quality scrum halves since the early days of Tommy Vile (Newport) and later Hayden Tanner (Swansea and Cardiff) but none of their gifted little men (and some like Gareth Edwards and Terry Holmes, not so little) have looked any more the part than Robert Nicholas Jones, who lit up an era of Welsh rugby that lacked the high success rate of previous times.

Jones had all the bits and pieces for a class scrum worker, being small but strong in calf and thigh with wonderfully quick hands to either flank, sharpness off the mark, exceptional punt control, a forest animal's instinct and that ability to operate at speed close to the ground. Nor did he shirk the unglamorous chores – these he adorned with gifts of anticipation that occasionally made it seem that he had hypnotised his adversary into doing what he wanted him to do.

His pace off the mark was never better demonstrated than in his thrilling try for Wales against Scotland at Murrayfield in 1995 when, within five minutes of kick-off, he was scuttling home underneath the

Scottish posts at the railway end of Murrayfield for the opening score.

Although Jones gained 54 caps for Wales, there were occasions when players of inferior ability were preferred to him so that, late in his career, he had a spell with Western Province in South Africa. He represented Wales in nine Five Nations Championships and played a major role in their Triple Crown and championship share success in 1988, but it must have been a disappointment that when Wales became the first winners of the Five Nations Championship trophy in 1984 he played in only one match and that as a replacement against Ireland. Yet he is one of the few Welsh players to have competed in all three World Cup competitions in 1987, 1991 and 1995, playing in 10 games and being Welsh scrum half when they won the third and fourth place play-off against Australia in the 1987 World Cup.

He captained Wales on five occasions, against New Zealand in 1989, and France, England, Scotland and Ireland in 1990. He made just the one Lions' tour –

to Australia in 1989 – but what a successful mission that turned out to be. He was directly opposed in the three Tests by the acknowledged outstanding scrum half in the world game, Nick Farr-Jones, and won their particular contest on points. There was quite a bit of niggle between those two but Jones never lost composure or grasp of his skill and ended the tour with his reputation fully established and, indeed, enhanced.

It undoubtedly helped Jones to keep his standards high that his rival and friend on the tour was Gary Armstrong (Jedforest and Scotland) who didn't have quite the pace of service but who, by his efforts in provincial games, kept up a strong challenge to Jones throughout the tour. Jones however played in all three Tests and it was a significant point that, having lost the first Test in Sydney by 30–12 (four tries to none) the Lions turned it round by winning the second and third Tests 19–12 and 19–18 when Jones was partnered by Rob Andrew (Wasps and England), each a clever tactician, each a master of tactical punting. The lad from Trebanos was a star turn with the Lions down under.

1989. Robert Jones sets up an attack against New South Wales and (*below*) clears the ball from the base of the scrum.

SCRUM HALF

C.D. MORRIS

Liverpool, Orrell

ENGLAND

Born 9 February 1964, Crickhowell
6ft – 13st 7lbs

26 caps for England
first versus Australia 1988
last versus France 1995 (World Cup)

British Lions – 1 tour, 3 Tests
1993 – New Zealand (1,2,3)

SCRUM HALF

Colin Dewi Morris came within one score of placing himself in the history books alongside only four famous predecessors – Carston Catcheside (Percy Park and England), Johnny Wallace (Oxford University and Scotland), Patrick Estève (Narbonne and France) and Philippe Sella (Agen and France). They are the only players to have scored a try in each of the four internationals in a Five Nations Championship. Morris scored tries against Scotland, Ireland and France in England's 1992 Five Nations campaign but in the last game against Wales at Twickenham, was unable to complete the quartet.

He was a pugnacious competitor, biggish for a scrum half and one who frequently asked questions of opposing fringe defenders and who also impressed with his mazy style of running in broken play. He was a clever tactician capable of providing an amalgam of serve, punt and probe whilst also being a ferocious tackler.

Morris had a dual qualification, having been born in Crickhowell in Wales and received his education at Brecon High School then at Alsager College. He had the distinction of having shot from junior rugby to a cap within nine months, having played for Winnington Park before joining Liverpool in 1983 then Orrell in 1989.

His was something of a mercurial international experience for, having scored a debut try in England's 28–19 win over the Wallabies at Twickenham on 5 November 1988 and played throughout the 1989 Five Nations Championship, he then missed 14 cap internationals. He finally made his return against Scotland in 1992 – the first of three comebacks that underlined his resilience and dogged persistence.

For his 26 caps he partnered Rob Andrew on 23 occasions, Stuart Barnes twice and Mike Catt once. He was on England's bench on 20 occasions. His only other international try was scored in the 33–16 defeat of South Africa at Twickenham on 14 November 1992. His great rival for the England scrum half berth was Richard Hill (Bath).

His performances in the 1993 Five Nations propelled him into the Lions' squad to tour New Zealand that year. His scrum half rival there was Robert Jones, but Morris played in all three Tests with Rob Andrew as his partner and also played in the games against North Harbour, New Zealand Maoris, Southland, Otago and Auckland. He shared in the outstanding rally of the tour when the Lions, 0–20 down to the Maoris, battled back to win by 24–20. In the Tests, however, the Lions' tight forwards disappointed but Morris was one of those who contributed handsomely to the Lions' reputation as a very popular touring party. Although the Lions won only seven of 13 games, it was significant that Morris was one of four players who were rated by the media to have had very impressive tours, the others being Ben Clarke, Scott Gibbs and Nick Popplewell.

During the Lions' tour of South Africa in 1997, Morris acted as a perceptive studio analyst for the Sky television channel.

1993. Rory Underwood provides some protection for Dewi Morris in the first Test against New Zealand.

M.J.S. DAWSON

Northampton

ENGLAND

Born 31 October 1972, Birkenhead
5ft 11in – 13st

14 caps for England
first versus Western Samoa 1995
still playing

British Lions – 1 tour, 3 Tests
1997 – South Africa (1,2,3)

SCRUM HALF

Whenever rugby folk discuss the career of Matthew James Sutherland Dawson of Northampton, inevitably that special try will dominate the conversation, the try that swung the first Test in favour of the 1997 British Lions in South Africa and really gave them the confidence to go on and win the Test series by 2–1.

It was an astonishing try that really shouldn't have been scored – but such was the perfection of everything Dawson did that he hoodwinked a bevy of South African defenders with as cheeky a scoring run as you ever will see. It was direct from a set piece, too, because from a scrummage outside the South African 22 and a scrummage that didn't tilt to the right to give Dawson a flying start, the Northampton scrum half picked up and took off at such a lick, but also at such an angle, that even that splendid South African flanker, Ruben Kruger, couldn't get enough grip on him. An outrageous one-handed dummy pass inside checked the South African captain, Gary Teichmann, as well as their scrum half, Joost van der Westhuizen, who was totally

deceived by the dummy. The South African left wing had already been left in the wake of Dawson who sprinted home to give the Lions the lead they never lost.

That try was typical of Dawson's style. He is versatile and a live wire, not afraid to ask questions of opposing fringe defenders and with intuitive selection of when to go and what path to take. Yet his inclusion on that Lions' tour was something of a surprise because he was number four in England at the time. Just before the selection was made he had not even been in England's squad of 21 players. Austin Healey (Leicester), Kieran Bracken (Bristol) and Andy Gomersall (Wasps) all seemed above him in the pecking order. Even at the start of the tour Dawson was expected to rate number three behind Rob Howley (Cardiff) and Healey. But when Howley suffered a shoulder dislocation and had to return home from the tour Dawson played in the three Tests and four other games, scored three tries, two in Test matches, and adjusted his pass beautifully for the Jeremy Guscott drop goal that clinched the second Test and the series.

Some reckoned that Dawson's selection for the tour owed much to the fact that his two Northampton club mates, Gregor Townsend and Paul Grayson, with each of whom he had formed a half back partnership, were to be on the tour as well. But whilst Howley was a big miss, Dawson fitted in well, didn't let the occasional error upset his focus and performed throughout with verve and resolve.

A former pupil of the Royal Grammar School, High Wycombe, he played 11 seasons from the age of seven with the Marlow club, representing the England Schools 18 Group as scrum half against Australia, France, Ireland, Scotland and Wales in 1990-91, played as a centre for England Under 21, was a wicket-keeper for Buckinghamshire and skilled enough in foot work to play schoolboy football for Chelsea. At one time he wasn't a bad rugby goal-kicker as well!

In May and June 1993 Dawson toured Canada with England but had the wretched luck to suffer hamstring damage after 10 minutes of the first match against British Columbia and missed the rest of the tour. He also toured with England A in Australia during the summer of 1995.

He was a teacher at Spratton Hall School in Northampton, and it was his Northampton alliance with Paul Grayson as his stand-off that so marked his first cap appearance against Western Samoa at Twickenham on 16 December 1995. They were the 50th pair of club half backs to represent England at cap level and David Hands wrote in *The Times* that 'it was the display of the Northampton halves on their debuts that was the brightest part of the England game. Would that older hands could have been as organised and effective as Grayson, as bouncy as Dawson'. England won 27–9 and the Grayson-Dawson partnership then operated in all four games of the 1996 Five Nations Championship. Of those, only that against France was lost, but Dawson then missed eight cap internationals before being restored for the match against Australia in Sydney a week after the end of the Lions' tour. Dawson and Grayson also were partners against Scotland and Ireland in England's 1998 Triple Crown success.

Before the tour, the former Lions' captain, John Dawes, had rated Dawson as 'busy, hard working and resilient'. He proved to be all of those and more as a Lion.

1997. Matt Dawson dives over for his second try of the series in the final Test against South Africa at Ellis Park.

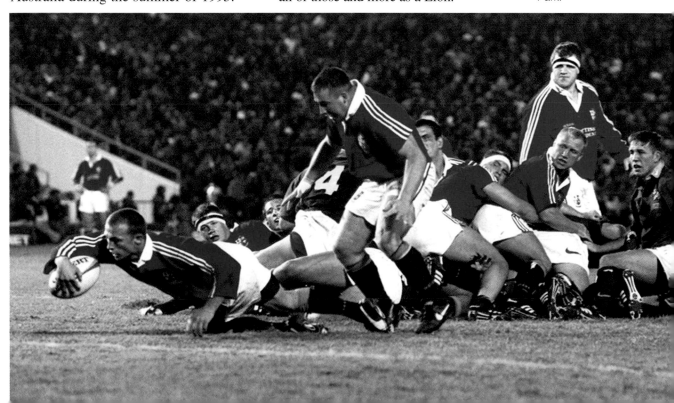

Arguably the best team builders in the business...

www.michaelpage.com

Michael Page
INTERNATIONAL
Specialist Recruitment Consultants

Australia · China · France · Germany · Hong Kong · Italy · Netherlands · New Zealand · Singapore · Spain · UK · USA

THE
FRONT ROW

J. McLAUCHLAN

Jordanhill College

SCOTLAND

Born 14 April 1947, Tarbolton
5ft 9¹/₂ in – 15st 6lbs

43 caps for Scotland
first versus England 1969
last versus New Zealand 1979

British Lions – 2 tours, 8 Tests
1971 – New Zealand (1,2,3,4)
1974 – South Africa (1,2,3,4)

It was no coincidence that Scottish and Lions' scrummaging was at its most effective in the seventies when a tough, rotund Scottish prop, John (Ian) McLauchlan was at the height of his powers. At only 5 feet 9¹/₂ inches and, initially, just under 14 stones which eventually was boosted to just over 15 stones, McLauchlan was rated by many as just too wee for the hurly burly of international scrummaging. How wrong they were.

A hard little fellow from Ayrshire, it was as a student of physical education at Jordanhill College in Glasgow that McLauchlan came under the guidance of Bill Dickinson, later to become Scotland's first coach (or advisor to the captain as he was then known). Dickinson was a scrummage specialist in body and feet positioning and in methods of easing and exerting scrummage pressure. With such a mentor McLauchlan soon became the scourge of opposing prop forwards as a rock solid loose-head, comfortable packing against just one shoulder and capable of creating all kinds of discomfort for the opposition. To give one example, he was a cornerstone of the successful Lions' pack in New Zealand in 1971, even against a far bigger opposite number in 'Jazz' Muller. There was one famous picture of McLauchlan actually hanging out to dry an 18-stone South African prop in the Lions' tour of 1974. No wonder he was given the nickname 'Mighty Mouse' McLauchlan.

He was a key member also of perhaps the finest Scottish pack of all time when, with his Glasgow colleague, Sandy Carmichael, he proved the bulwark of the Scottish eights of the seventies – McLauchlan, Frank Laidlaw, Carmichael, Alastair McHarg, Gordon Brown, Nairn McEwan, Peter Brown and Roger Arneil.

He captained Scotland in 19 cap internationals as well as against Argentina in 1973 and Tonga in 1974. Ten of those internationals were won, including shock Murrayfield victories over the might of Wales in 1973 and 1975 and of England in 1974 and 1976.

McLauchlan had the quiet conviction that no other prop could trouble him and he set about proving that in every grade of play. His first cap international assignment was to take on Coventry's Keith Fairbrother, followed by South Africa's equally formidable Hannes Marais. McLauchlan more than survived.

It was something of an injustice that during his lengthy tenure as Scotland's first choice loose-head no Triple Crown, outright championship or Grand Slam was gathered in, yet McLauchlan was an integral part of several famous Scottish wins as was his side-kick Carmichael with whom he propped Scotland's scrummage on 34 cap occasions.

He toured with Scotland in Argentina in 1969, Australia in 1970, New Zealand in 1975 (when he was the only one to play in all seven games) and the Far East in 1977. He played close on 20 seasons with Jordanhill College and notched up a record 69 games for Glasgow. He played his last cap international against the All Blacks at Murrayfield in 1979 when he was 37 years old.

He exuded a quiet confidence that inspired colleagues, never more than on his two Lions' tours. Chosen as prospective understudy to the Irish strong man, Ray McLoughlin, in New Zealand 1971, he had to take over the lead role when McLoughlin (and Carmichael) were injured in a nasty match against Canterbury. McLauchlan played in 16 of the 24 games and in all four Tests and scored the only try in the Lions' 9–3 first win in Dunedin. In South Africa with the Lions in 1974 he played in 13 of the 22 games and in all four Tests when he was opposed again by Hannes Marais. So McLauchlan had the distinction of holding down a key role in the two most successful Lions' tours of all times.

It is fascinating to contemplate how McLauchlan would have fared against some of the giant props of the modern game: on his seventies' form, without a lot of bother!

1974. Ian McLauchlan provides protection for his front row partner Fran Cotton in the game against Northern Transvaal.

F.E. COTTON

Loughborough Colleges, Coventry, Sale

ENGLAND

Born 3 January 1947, Wigan
6ft 2in – 16st 7lbs

31 caps for England
first versus Scotland 1971
last versus Wales 1981

British Lions – 3 tours, 7 Tests
1974 – South Africa (1,2,3,4)
1977 – New Zealand (2,3,4)
1980 – South Africa

Some reckoned that at six feet two inches and with the build of a water buffalo, Francis Edward Cotton was just too big for the front row and especially for the loose-head berth. But the big man from Wigan proved them all wrong by developing into a mighty scrummager on both loose- and tight-head, and that at the very highest level of play, with the British Lions.

There was, of course, much more to Cotton than that. That he was no slouch when he stepped on the accelerator and was also possessed of high grade handling skills was underlined at the first World Sevens tournament held as part of the SRU Centenary season on 7 April 1973. Cotton captained the England Seven who carried all before them in beating Ireland in the final by 22–18.

Cotton, of course, was a physical education graduate of Loughborough Colleges. Although his father was a successful rugby league player, Cotton took up the rugby union game at Newton-Le-Willows Grammar School and so developed his potential as to be first capped against Scotland in 1971 when

still a student. He had already impressed the national selectors in the England Under 25 side against the 1970 Fijians.

Having been on standby for the Lions' tour to New Zealand in 1971, Cotton captained the North-West Counties to their 16–14 win over the touring All Blacks at Workington, the first time an English regional side had ever beaten the All Blacks. He was an influential figure again when the Northern Division beat Graham Mourie's All Blacks by 21–9 at Otley on 17 November 1979. When England wrapped up their 1980 Grand Slam with a 30–18 defeat of Scotland at Murrayfield, Cotton became England's most capped prop with 30, a position now tenanted by Jason Leonard with 63. Cotton also captained England against Ireland, Wales and France in 1975.

He represented England at both loose-head and tight-head and did the same for the Lions. In South Africa in 1974 he played in 14 of the 22 games and all four Tests as tight-head and was captain in the 20–16 win over the Quaggas. In New Zealand in 1977 he appeared in 16 of the 26 games, including

LOOSE HEAD

three of the four Tests as loose-head, and was captain in the 13–11 defeat of Hawke's Bay. As a PE specialist he was a valuable aide in the forwards' fitness sessions.

It was in the sixth match of the Lions' tour of South Africa in 1980, his third tour, when the opposition were the South African Federation XV, that Cotton was stretchered from the field suffering from chest pains which caused heavy anxiety among the medical staff. His absence proved a big loss to the Lions but it was testimony to his determination and perseverance that he made a comeback for England against Wales in 1981. Sadly he suffered injury, having to be replaced after just 15 minutes, and leg problems thus ended his international career.

Cotton's success with the Lions continued, however, when he created a superb management team with Ian McGeechan and Jim Telfer in 1997 for the South African tour. The Lions won the Test series 2–1 against the Springboks. Cotton, indeed, had proved a big man in every respect. Recently he has been Vice-Chairman (Playing) of the Rugby Football Union.

1977. Derek Quinnell watches as Fran Cotton moves the ball out during the Lions' first-ever match on home soil. The game against the Barbarians was part of the Queen's Silver Jubilee celebrations.

D.M.B. SOLE

Bath, Edinburgh Academicals

SCOTLAND

Born 8 May 1962, Aylesbury
5ft 11in – 15st 10lbs

44 caps for Scotland
first versus France 1986
last versus Australia 1992

British Lions – 1 tour, 3 Tests
1989 – Australia (1,2,3)

LOOSE HEAD

No Scot who was there on 17 March 1990 will ever forget that moment of drama when David Michael Barclay Sole walked the Scottish team on to Murrayfield for the Grand Slam decider with England in a spirit of defiance that lit the touch paper to arguably Scotland's greatest display – they pipped the 'auld enemy' to the Slam by 13–7. It wasn't the first time that Sole, Scotland's captain on a record 25 occasions, had been party to an unexpected Scottish win over England. On 9 April 1980 at Nuneaton, he was in the Scottish Schools side that gained a shock 13–11 win over England Schools. The captain for Scotland that day was one Gavin Hastings.

Educated at Blairmore School in Aberdeenshire, Glenalmond in Perthshire and Exeter University, Sole developed into a modern style loose-head prop. He was a clever and strong if not notably destructive scrummager, highly mobile, indeed very quick by prop standards (even though, like most props, he did ride low in the water) and possessed of splendid handling skills that were underlined notably when he represented his university at the Middlesex Sevens. Never a game went by without Sole exhibiting yet again his immense value as a roving prop forward, putting in a shoal of copy book tackles. But he never lost sight of his priority obligations as a loose-head prop forward.

He first played for Bath against Bristol in 1984 and was in Bath's cup winning side in 1987. He was one of six new caps in Scotland's 18–17 defeat of France at Murrayfield in 1986, the others being Gavin and Scott Hastings, Matt Duncan, Jeremy Campbell-Lamerton and Finlay Calder. He played in 44 of 48 consecutive internationals, missing only the England, Ireland and Romania games of 1986 and being rested from the Zimbabwe game in the 1991 World Cup. In the 1987 and 1991 World Cups, when captain in the latter, he played in nine of the 10 games. He now stands second equal with Iain Milne (44) in Scotland's list of most capped props behind Sandy Carmichael (50).

Sole's leadership qualities were acknowledged not only by the Scotland selectors but also by the Lions and the Barbarians. On the Lions' tour of Australia in 1989, when he played in eight of the 12 games and in all three Tests in a Lions' series win by 2–1, he was captain in the matches against New South Wales B and the Anzac XV. He also led the Barbarians to their spirited 10–21 opposition to the touring All Blacks at Twickenham on 25 November 1989.

He represented Scotland in six Five Nations Championships, had some heated jousts with England's tight-head, Jeff Probyn, in particular, and made his mark as a gifted all round prop, capable of reaching the highest standard, no matter what the conditions or the opposition. He captained Scotland on their 1990 tour to New Zealand when, although beaten 18–21 by the All Blacks in the Test in Auckland, Scotland had the satisfaction of scoring two tries to one but going down to the boot of the inimitable Grant Fox. Sole also was captain when Scotland toured Australia in 1992, when he ended his international career. Having scored cap international tries against Romania 1989 and New Zealand 1990 it was in every sense appropriate that, in his very last cap international against the Wallabies in Brisbane on 21 June 1992, he should sign off by registering the last try of the match.

1989. David Sole makes the ball available in the first Test against Australia in Sydney.

N.J. POPPLEWELL

Greystones, Wasps, Newcastle

IRELAND

Born 6 April 1964, Dublin
5ft 10in – 17st 3lbs

48 caps for Ireland
first versus New Zealand 1989
still playing

British Lions – 1 tour, 3 Tests
1993 – New Zealand (1,2,3)

It isn't often that one comes across a schools hockey international who develops into a successful British Lions' prop forward, but that was the transition achieved by Nicholas John Popplewell who lies second with 44 caps to Phil Orr (58) in Ireland's list of most capped props.

As a pupil of Newtown Secondary School in Waterford, Popplewell represented Irish Schools at hockey before gaining his first club experience at rugby union with the Gorey Club in County Wexford. Later he joined Greystones in County Wicklow and played first for Leinster in 1987. Having represented Ireland Under 25 against Italy in 1987, he toured France with Ireland in 1988 and North America in 1989 when he played in both non-cap Tests. He was unlucky to be injured in his first cap international against the All Blacks in 1989 and thus missed the 1990 Five Nations Championship. But from the Namibia match at Windhoek in 1991 onwards, he played in 43 of the next 47 internationals, missing only the Japan match in the 1991 World Cup

when he was rested and the two Tests against Australia in 1994 when he had to miss the tour to have an operation on cruciate knee ligaments.

Popplewell proved a worthy successor to previous Ireland and Lions' props such as Tom Clifford, Syd Millar, Ray McLoughlin, Sean Lynch and Phil Orr. He had the ideal build – stocky, strong, barrel-chested and powerful in upper body and in undercarriage – but also exceptional mobility that enabled him to reach parts of the pitch that were beyond other denizens of the front row.

Having captained Leinster, he also led Ireland in the 1995 World Cup defeat of Japan by 50–28 in Bloemfontein. He played in three of the four games of the 1991 World Cup for two tries against Zimbabwe and in the 1995 World Cup in South Africa he played in all four games, against New Zealand, Japan, Wales and France.

Ireland were unable to claim championship or Triple Crown honours during his spell in the 1992, 1993, 1994, 1995 and 1996 Five Nations Championships but he shared in the

LOOSE HEAD

shock 13–12 defeat of England at Twickenham in 1994. Popplewell's rating as one of the world's most effective loose-head prop forwards was mirrored in his switch from Greystones to Wasps in 1994, then to Newcastle in 1995.

His mobility and handling and running expertise were underlined in his distinction of being chosen four times for the Barbarians against major touring sides – Australia 1992 and 1996, New Zealand 1993 and South Africa 1994. In the last of those matches he was part of an all-Irish front row of Popplewell, Keith Wood and Peter Clohessy; the Barbarians defeated those 1994 South Africans by 23–15 at Lansdowne Road.

With the 1993 Lions in New Zealand he played in seven of the 13 games and was the only Irish player in all three

Tests, when he was directly opposed to arguably the finest tight-head in the world, Olo Brown of Auckland. Five players were reckoned to have performed particularly well during that tour – the captain Gavin Hastings, Ben Clarke, Scott Gibbs, Dewi Morris and Nicholas John Popplewell.

1993. The front row against the All Blacks, Nick Popplewell (right) with Brian Moore and Jason Leonard, and (*below*) a rampaging run from Popplewell in the Lions' glorious victory in the second Test at Wellington.

R.W. WINDSOR

Cross Keys, Pontypool

WALES

Born 31 January 1948, Newport
5ft 9in – 14st 9lbs

28 caps for Wales
first versus Australia 1973
last versus France 1979

British Lions – 2 tours, 5 Tests
1974 – South Africa (1,2,3,4)
1977 – New Zealand (1)

HOOKER

Whenever the name Robert William 'Bobby' Windsor enters the conversation inevitably memories will be revived of Pontypool and the 1974 British Lions' unbeaten record in South Africa that included winning the Test series by 3–0 with one draw.

Bobby Windsor was a remarkable character whether in club or international company, immensely popular with all his colleagues for his sharp wit and unfettered sense of humour. Whilst the Lions were slogging their way through the disappointments of New Zealand in 1977, not least the constant rain and muddy pitches (even though they lost only one game outside the Tests, and that to New Zealand Universities), it was the cheery Windsor who helped to keep the Lions smiling with his sense of fun. In fact he himself didn't quite reach in New Zealand the same quality of performance that he had done with the Lions in South Africa three years previously.

Naturally imbued with the physical hardness of a steel worker, Windsor was guided along the paths of technical excellence by the inimitable Ray Prosser, his mentor at Pontypool and himself a former Lion in Australia and New Zealand in 1959, when he had played in the final Test against New Zealand which the Lions won by 9–6. Windsor had started out as a stand-off and full back for the Newport Schools XV out of Brynglas Secondary Modern School in Newport.

Formerly with Cross Keys, Windsor became a much respected part of the Pontypool scene, serving the club throughout his international career and following that as coach and elder citizen. He played in Pontypool's 1973 and 1975 championship-winning sides and it was with that club that he created a renowned front row partnership with Charlie Faulkner (previously also of Cross Keys) and Graham Price. They were a formidable trio with the immense strength and solid worth of the props set alongside Windsor's hooking expertise, accurate throwing and his strength in field coverage and maul. They played together as the Welsh front row in 19 cap internationals and when Faulkner joined

1974. Bobby Windsor (centre) watches as fellow members of the front five – Gordon Brown, Fran Cotton, Willie John McBride and Ian McLauchlan – look after their scrum half and (*below*) **1977**, in Fiji at the end of his second Lions tour.

the 1977 Lions in New Zealand as a replacement, it gave huge pleasure to all at the Park in Pontypool when the famous trio played together for the Lions against Bay of Plenty, Counties and Thames Valley and against Fiji in Suva.

A try-scoring hooker, Windsor scored over 30 tries for Pontypool in the three seasons 1976, 1977 and 1978. He also scored a debut try in his very first international appearance against Australia, in 1973. He gained 28 caps in a row in the Five Nations Championships of 1974, 1975, 1976, 1977, 1978 and 1979, during which Wales won two Grand Slams, four Triple Crowns and four championships. In most of those he was partnered with his Pontypool buddies, Faulkner and Price.

As one of the nine Welshmen in the 1974 Lions' squad in South Africa, Windsor played in 13 of the 22 games and in all four Tests when his props were Ian McLauchlan (Scotland) and Fran Cotton (England). There were 18 Welshmen in the 1977 Lions' tour to New Zealand where Windsor played in 13 of the 26 games, but in only the first Test which the Lions lost in Wellington by 16–12. Peter Wheeler (England) played in the remaining three Tests with Fran Cotton and Graham Price as his props but 'the Duke', as Windsor was known to all his Lions' teammates, had already gained the respect of friend and foe alike as one of the greats from Pontypool Park.

HOOKER

P.J. WHEELER

Leicester

ENGLAND

Born 26 November 1948, London
5ft 11in – 14st 2lbs

41 caps for England
first versus France 1975
last versus Wales 1984

British Lions – 2 tours, 7 Tests
1977 – New Zealand (2,3,4)
1980 – South Africa (1,2,3,4)

HOOKER

Over the years England has produced a line of tough bulldog type hookers who have made a huge impact on the game at all levels – among them Bert Toft, Eric Evans, Sam Hodgson, John Pullin and Brian Moore. Undoubtedly one who would be rated by many as the most successful of all has been that devoted Tiger from Welford Road, Peter John Wheeler, who lies 12th in the list of most capped Englishmen with 41.

Wheeler was a tough, talented technician, disinclined to take a backward step even in the physically demanding environs of the front row and even against the hardest of rivals. His basics were secure and he revelled in the unglamorous chores whilst asserting himself to advantage in broken play exchanges.

Having been educated at Brockley County School in London he played three seasons with Old Brockleians until his work in insurance took him to Leicester, where he joined the Tigers in 1969. He had toured in the Far East with England and had been standby hooker for the Lions

in South Africa in 1974 before being awarded his first cap under Fran Cotton's captaincy against France at Twickenham in February 1975. In the next game against Wales he was injured and replaced by his rival, John Pullin, who played in the next three internationals. Wheeler, however, gave such an impressive display against the touring Wallabies, with four tight-head strikes in England's 23–6 win at Twickenham on 3 January 1976, as to establish himself as Pullin's successor with 27 consecutive cap appearances from the Scotland game in 1977 onwards.

Wheeler developed into a natural leader, captaining Leicester to four consecutive knock-out cup finals, of which three were won, and leading the Midlands Division to victories over Australia in 1981, Fiji in 1982 and New Zealand in 1983. Having also captained England to their 15–9 win over the touring All Blacks on 19 November 1983, he led his country in the 1984 Five Nations Championship and was 35 years old when he played his last cap international against Wales at Twickenham in 1984. In that match he was accompanied in the England team by five other men of Leicester – Dusty Hare, Clive Woodward, Rory Underwood, Les Cusworth and Nick Youngs.

Although England had just one notable success during Wheeler's 10 seasons of Five Nations Championship play it was one to be treasured – England's first Grand Slam for 23 years, when Wheeler formed arguably England's most formidable front row with Fran Cotton and Phil Blakeway in all four games, in 1980.

Not altogether surprisingly nicknamed 'Brace', Wheeler rose to the challenge of Lions' selection when, in New Zealand in 1977, he played in 13 of the 26 games and in three of the four Tests, having been one of five changes in the Lions' pack for the second Test, taking over from Bobby Windsor. Wheeler scored a try against the South Mid-Canterbury and North Otago XV and was one of five Lions rated as having given 'consistently fine performances'. That Lions' pack was reckoned by some to be the best ever, consisting as it did of Cotton, Wheeler, Price, Beaumont, Brown, Quinnell or Squire, Duggan and Cobner or Neary. With the Lions in South Africa in 1980 Wheeler played in 11 of the 18 games and in all four Tests with Clive Williams and Fran Cotton as his props. He scored a timely try in the 21–17 defeat of Orange Free State.

He was always liable to score a try here and there. For the Barbarians against East Midlands in the Hobbs Memorial match at Northampton on 7 March 1974 he scored three.

1980. Peter Wheeler in the thick of things against South Africa in the third Test at Port Elizabeth.

B.C. MOORE

Nottingham, Harlequins

ENGLAND

Born 11 January 1962, Birmingham
5ft 9in – 14st 2lbs

64 caps for England
first versus Scotland 1987
last versus Western Samoa 1995 (R)

British Lions – 2 tours, 5 Tests
1989 – Australia (1,2,3)
1993 – New Zealand (2,3)

HOOKER

No player ever epitomised more the English bulldog spirit than Brian Christopher Moore, whose whole being on a rugby field oozed aggression and challenge and refusal to contemplate defeat. Apart from being an admirable motivator in his attitude and style, he was also a typical modern hooker: strong in frame to withstand the buffetings of the front row, technically dependable as ball-winner and ball-channeller, accurate in line-out throwing and with educated hands, so that he made a big contribution as a link man in open play attack. He could step on the gas as well!

Even in his early days he had good hands as, for instance, when he captained the Nottingham squad to the Middlesex Sevens final in both 1985 and 1986. Having been educated at Crossley and Porter High School in Halifax and having gained his law degree at the University of Nottingham, he captained England Students, played first for Moseley in 1981, represented Notts-Lincs-Derbys in the County Championship final of 1985 and also captained England B the same year.

Moore became England's most capped forward with 64, to which can be added five Lions' Test appearances. He has the notable distinction of having played in all 33 Five Nations Championship games since his first appearance against Scotland in 1987 and his last in the championship against Scotland in 1995. Of those 33 only five were lost. In his entire international career he missed only six of 70 games.

He also made his mark as England's hooker in all three of their Grand Slams in 1991, 1992 and 1995 and he was still as lively as ever at going on 34, when he played his last cap international out of the Harlequins club as a replacement against Western Samoa at Twickenham on 16 December 1995.

Moore's amazing durability was also underlined when he played in all three World Cup competitions in 1987, 1991 and 1995. In the first two he played in eight of the 10 games, including the final against Australia in 1991, missing only the two USA matches. In South Africa in 1995 he was one of only five English players to take part in all six

World Cup games when England lost the play-off match to France. The others were Mike Catt, Rory Underwood, Martin Johnson and Tim Rodber.

His unquenchable spirit had much to do with the British Lions' recovery from one Test down to the Wallabies in 1989 to a series win by 2–1. In some rough and at times bitter exchanges Moore set a strong example in commitment and defiance and self-belief, not to mention in verbal encouragement to his colleagues. He played in seven of the 12 games and in a splendid Lions' forward effort had David Sole (Scotland) and David Young (Wales)

as his props in all three Tests. On the Lions' tour of New Zealand in 1993 he featured in seven of the 13 games and, having been left out of the first Test, was then paired with Nick Popplewell (Ireland) and Jason Leonard (England) in the second which the Lions won to square the series, and also in the third when the Lions led 10–0 but eventually lost by 13–30.

Moore has played some 16 seasons of senior rugby and only one hooker in the world game has gained more caps – his old adversary, Sean Fitzpatrick of New Zealand, with 92, and who has just announced his retirement.

1993. The unquenchable spirit of Brian Moore.

HOOKER

K.G.M. WOOD

Garryowen, Harlequins

IRELAND

Born 27 January 1972, Limerick
6ft – 16st 5lbs

17 caps for Ireland
first versus Australia 1994
still playing

British Lions – 1 tour, 2 Tests
1997 – South Africa (1,2)

They might have called him 'the demon barber of Limerick' for it was Keith Gerard Mallinson Wood who gave Ian McGeechan, the Lions' coach, his (very) short-back-and-sides haircut as a result of a bet on the 1997 Lions winning the Test series in South Africa. The Irish hooker seemed to enjoy the experience, perhaps partly because he is not himself over-endowed with plumage!

He showed on tour, however, that he is well endowed with spirit, resolution, skill, dogged perseverance and acceleratory power that has taken sundry opponents by surprise. He has been described as a hooker playing as a flanker and assuredly he covers the paddock in swashbuckling, physical and uncompromising fashion, and sometimes gets to parts where hookers are not expected to be. He frequently just explodes into the action prior to displaying hidden talent. In the crucial second Test for the Lions against South Africa it was Wood who suddenly burst up the touch line then, of all things for a hooker, kicked ahead to perfection without breaking stride, thus igniting the move that, with a little help from Gregor Townsend and Matt Dawson, both of Northampton, set up Jeremy Guscott for the drop goal that clinched the series.

Wood is a chip off the old block, for his father, Gordon, also out of the Garryowen club in Limerick, played 29 times for Ireland as well as two Tests for the 1959 Lions in New Zealand. Educated at that famous rugby nursery, St Munchins College, in Limerick and at the University of Limerick, Wood junior is a former customer advisor with the Irish Permanent plc and had previously excelled at swimming and hurling. He was a member of the Garryowen sides who won the All Ireland League in 1992 and 1994, played for Ireland Under 21 in 1992-93 (including the match against the formidable New Zealand Youth at Donnybrook in October 1993), became established in the Munster side in 1993-94 having been on the Irish bench for the first time against Australia in October 1992, and played his first game for Ireland A against Scotland A in December 1993.

HOOKER

He created a sensational impact on Ireland's tour of Australia in 1994, so much so as to gain preference over his Munster rival, Terry Kingston (Dolphin), for the two Tests. The Irish lost them, but not without restoring their pride and prestige with spirited displays. *Rothmans Rugby Yearbook* recorded that Keith Wood impressed in the Tests with his all round skills and pace in the loose. Wood played in four of the eight games but was injured in the first game against Western Australia.

There is no doubt that he would have gained far more than his 17 caps but for injuries, notably to his shoulder which was dislocated several times and eventually required surgery. From Wood's first cap against the Wallabies he played five cap internationals in a row, missed the next four, was back for the World Cup in South Africa in 1995 but put out his shoulder against Japan in Bloemfontein. He missed a further nine cap internationals but a week after playing for Ireland A against South Africa A in November 1996 he was restored to the national side against the touring Wallabies and made captain. He led Ireland against Australia and Italy in 1996

and against France on 18 January 1997 but was injured again in the French game and replaced after 38 minutes. There was concern that that injury would keep him out of the Lions' tour but clearly the Lions' management saw him as potentially a hugely influential figure, so out he went. He was by then a member of the Harlequins club and formed their impressive front row with Jason Leonard and Frenchman Laurent Benezech. He had already tasted victory over the Springboks for the Barbarians at Lansdowne Road by 23–15 on 3 December 1994, when the Baa-Baas played an all Ireland front row – Nick Popplewell, Wood and Peter Clohessy.

Wood was a popular figure in the Lions' party and was described by Derek Douglas of the *Glasgow Herald* as 'combining raw aggression with great ingenuity'. However, he suffered injury in the first game against Eastern Province and in the fourth against Mpumalanga, but he played in the splendid 42–12 win over Natal and in the first and second Tests which were won. Still only 26, Wood, who has captained Ireland in nine cap internationals, should be a significant figure for Ireland and the Lions for some time to come.

1997. The front row in the first Test against South Africa at Newlands: Phil Wallace, Keith Wood and Tom Smith.

J.F. LYNCH

St Mary's College

IRELAND

Born 22 September 1942, Dublin
6ft – 15st 4lbs

17 caps for Ireland
first versus France 1971
last versus New Zealand 1974

British Lions – 1 tour, 4 Tests
1971 – Australia/New Zealand (1,2,3,4)

TIGHT HEAD

'Cometh the hour, cometh the man' could well be applied with justification to John Francis (Sean) Lynch who, along with his Scottish colleague Ian McLauchlan (Jordanhill College), stepped into the breach during the Lions' 1971 tour in Australia and New Zealand. They proved to be key elements in the first Lions' Test series triumph this century.

The two first choice props on that famous tour were Sandy Carmichael (Scotland) and Ray McLoughlin (Ireland) but both were injured in a nasty game against Canterbury shortly before the first Test, Carmichael suffering a multiple fracture of his cheekbone. So McLauchlan and Lynch, with John Pullin (England) as hooker, had to withstand the combined scrummaging efforts of the giant Jazz Muller, Tane Norton and Richie Guy in the four Tests. They did so with such success that technical superiority in the scrummage became a powerful offensive weapon for the Lions who won 23 of their 26 games and lost only

two – the very first against Queensland, 11–15 in Brisbane, and the second New Zealand Test in Christchurch, 12–22. Lynch played in 15 of those 26 games and was a popular member of the party.

He had been the first player, along with Dennis Hickie, from the St Mary's College club in Dublin to be capped by Ireland. He was a late developer in cap terms, as he was 28 years old when awarded his first against France in 1971. His role was as a sapping, disruptive scrummager with great strength in arms and shoulders. He then played in 10 internationals in a row before Roger Clegg (Bangor) was preferred for the French match of 1973. Lynch was soon restored, however, after showing splendid form in the final trial in January 1974 and he went on to play in the Five Nations Championship that followed and also against the President's XV. He was 32 when he gained his last cap against Ian Kirkpatrick's All Blacks at Lansdowne Road on 23 November 1974. He was sometimes referred to as a baby-faced tough guy, and tough he assuredly

1971.
Sean Lynch
(centre)
celebrates
Peter Dixon's
try in the final
Test in
Auckland.

was. In the Lions' match against the New Zealand Maoris in 1977 his lip was split open so badly that it required 14 stitches: yet he missed only three games and showed unfettered resolution and spirit against the West Coast-Buller XV on his return in time for the first Test.

Lynch had captained St Mary's College to the Leinster Cup in April in 1969 and unusually was given the captaincy of Leinster on his provincial debut against Connaught in November 1969. It was as a late deputy for the much-capped Syd Millar, who was ill, that Lynch stated his international credentials against Argentina in 1970. He was at loose-head on that occasion but operated at tight-head almost throughout his international and Lions' career as well as for Leinster, when they held the All Blacks to 3–8 at Lansdowne Road on 13 November 1974 and when Ireland limited those All Blacks to one try in the 6–15 defeat at Lansdowne Road 10 days later.

A licensed vintner with a pub in Dublin, Lynch shared in Ireland's Five Nations Championship success in 1974 when he formed a formidable front row with Ray McLoughlin and Ken Kennedy. They had Willie John McBride and Moss Keane behind them. That was some Irish tight five.

TIGHT HEAD

G. PRICE

Pontypool

WALES

Born 24 November 1951, Egypt
5ft 11in – 15st 2lbs

41 caps for Wales
first versus France 1975
last versus France 1983

British Lions – 3 tours, 12 Tests
1977 – New Zealand (1,2,3,4)
1980 – South Africa (1,2,3,4)
1983 – New Zealand (1,2,3,4)

TIGHT HEAD

It has been given to few prop forwards to celebrate their debut cap international by hacking and chasing over 75 yards for a spectacular try late in the game to clinch a shock victory – but that is how Graham Price of Pontypool launched his cap career when Wales beat France 25–10 at Parc des Princes on 18 January 1975. That was the first of his four cap tries: he scored a second against France in 1980 and two against Japan on Wales's tour of the Far East in 1975. From the day of that first cap Price played in 41 of 42 consecutive cap internationals, missing only the Scotland game in 1983, and established himself as arguably the best tight-head prop in the world game.

As an engineer he was naturally strong and so developed his scrummage prowess and his ball sense as to become a rounded forward of much skill, although the scrummage grinding process to which he subjected his opposite numbers was a Price hallmark. Of course he became a member of the famous Pontypool front row along with Charlie Faulkner and Bobby Windsor who owed a lot to the coaching of the former British Lions' prop, Ray Prosser, and who were dubbed by Max Boyce as the 'Viet Gwent'. Educated at Jones West Monmouth Grammar School in Pontypool and at the University of Wales Institute of Science and Technology, Price played for Pontypool when still at school. He also played five games for the Welsh Schools 19 Group. He followed a former pupil of the school, Bryn Meredith, into the Welsh and Lions' front rows.

A quiet, modest personality, Price refused to be provoked into indiscipline even when his jaw was broken in the Wales versus Australia international in 1988 or when his eye was damaged in a French match. The Welshman simply let his quality as a hard-grafting prop do the talking for him and thus became the most respected tight-head in the world game.

A permanent fixture in the Welsh side, he first broke Denzil Williams's record of 36 caps for a Welsh prop, then in the Wales versus England game at Cardiff on

1977. The Pontypool front row – Graham Price, Bobby Windsor and Charlie Faulkner – in Lions' colours against Bay of Plenty.

TIGHT HEAD

5 February 1983 he won his 39th cap to beat the record for a Welsh forward held by Mervyn Davies. For the moment Price lies 11th in the all-time Welsh caps list.

In New Zealand in 1977 he started a run of 12 consecutive Lions' Tests, a record for a front row forward. He played in 14 of the 26 games and was the only front row man to survive following the first Test, having Phil Orr and Bobby Windsor as his front row colleagues then, followed by Fran Cotton and Peter Wheeler in the other three. Price was described as having been 'an outstanding tight-head throughout the tour' and as 'having played magnificently in the fourth Test'.

The 1980 Lions had a nightmare series of injuries in South Africa and Price played in 12 of the 18 games including the four Tests, in which Clive Williams and Peter Wheeler were his front row colleagues. Price scored a try in the 21–15 defeat of Natal and the only Lions' try in the first Test which the tourists lost 22–26. In New Zealand 1983 he figured in 10 of the 18 games and all four Tests, in three of which the loose-head prop was his Pontypool colleague, Staff Jones.

It seems scant reward for all of his admirable efforts that all three Lions' Test series were lost 10–2 but there was consolation in the enhancement of his standing as a world class prop and in the fact that the Viet Gwent – Faulkner, Windsor and Price – were together for the Lions in 1977 against Counties-Thames Valley, Bay of Plenty and Fiji. They were pretty chuffed about that at Pontypool Park.

D. YOUNG

Swansea, Cardiff

WALES

Born 27 June 1967, Aberdare
6ft 1in – 17st 12lbs

28 caps for Wales
first versus England 1987
still playing

British Lions – 2 tours, 3 Tests
1989 – Australia (1,2,3)
1997 – South Africa

TIGHT HEAD

No Welsh rugby player ever had a more dramatic entry into a cap international for the very first time than David Young of Swansea and Cardiff. There he was, 19 years old and enjoying a spell of club rugby in Canberra, Australia, having paid his own fare out there when, out of the blue, came a call from the Welsh selectors for him to join their injury-hit World Cup squad in Australia and New Zealand in 1987.

He was thrown to the wolves to achieve his first cap in the quarter-final of that World Cup, in Brisbane against England. His immediate rival that day was the experienced Paul Rendall. He thus became the youngest Welsh prop international at 19 years and 11 months. Wales won 16–3. In the very next match, the semi-final, Young met the All Blacks head on in packing directly opposite Steve McDowell in the scrummage. The youngster, however, surprised everyone with his strength, hardness and scrummaging technique in both games and clearly fulfilled the considerable potential he had shown as a young player.

Educated at Aberdare Comprehensive School, he played for East Wales at Under 11 grade before representing Aberamman Youth, then as captain of Wales at Under 15, Under 16 and Youth levels before joining Swansea in 1987. He moved to Cardiff in the 1988-89 season.

Young has the ideal build for a tight-head prop, being exceptionally strong in back and hips and with a fetish for fitness that gives him impressive power and durability. It was hardly surprising that rugby league scouts became interested in him so that he joined Leeds Rugby League Club in 1990 and moved later to Salford. He made 13 rugby league appearances for Wales whilst also being captain of club and country in the then only professional game.

When the rugby union game was declared professional, Young was one of the first to return to it, rejoining Cardiff in the summer of 1996 after six years in rugby league. Clearly he had much to offer in experience and in skill development and he was restored to the Welsh side against the touring Wallabies at Cardiff Arms Park on 1 December 1996. He has now played in 14 of the last 18 cap internationals. Having been an influential figure when Wales won the Triple Crown and shared the Five Nations Championship with France in 1988, it was no surprise when he was selected for the British Lions' tour of Australia in 1989. There he revelled in the tough and sometimes bitter exchanges and in the aggressive, hard-nosed approach of the Lions' forwards. He figured in seven of the 12 games and played in all three Tests, along with David Sole (Scotland) and Brian Moore (England) as his front row colleagues. He was heavily criticised by the Australian media for alleged foul play on the Wallabies' line-out specialist, Steve Cutler, a rare lapse from a player respected for just getting on with the job of playing.

It spoke volumes for his ability to adapt quickly to the 15-a-side game on his return from rugby league that he was chosen to tour South Africa with the Lions in 1997. Although he was injured in the second tour match against Border and was not selected for the Test series which the Lions won by 2–1, he played a full part in the tour, appeared in six of the 13 games and notably was in the Lions' sides who gained super victories over Natal (42–12), Orange Free State (52–30) and Northern Orange Free State (67–39).

The Barbarians also recognised Young's all-round qualities by playing him along with his Lions' Test colleague, David Sole, against Australia in Cardiff on 26 November 1988 and against New Zealand at Twickenham on 25 November 1989.

1989. David Young (left) and David Sole prop Brian Moore in the first Test against Australia at Sydney.

J. LEONARD

Saracens, Harlequins

ENGLAND

Born 14 August 1968, Barking
5ft 10in – 17st 7lbs

63 caps for England
first versus Argentina 1990
still playing

British Lions – 2 tours, 3 Tests
1993 – New Zealand (2,3)
1997 – South Africa (1[R])

It was on 23 November 1996 that Jason Leonard was given the honour of leading England on to the field at Twickenham for the game against Italy, to mark his 50th cap. He was the seventh Englishman to achieve that milestone but the youngest at just 28. Not only that but he has missed only the Western Samoa match, when he was rested at the 1995 World Cup in South Africa, and the Argentina Tests in 1997 since his first cap against the Pumas on England's tour to Argentina in 1990. That first cap was gained 11 days before his 22nd birthday. Indeed at the present time Leonard has played in 63 of the last 67 cap internationals, a remarkable run pointing to his admirable zest, strength and durability and considering that, at one time, his career was threatened by a neck injury which required a bone graft. Of his 63 caps, 51 have been as a loose-head and 12 as a tight-head and he has operated in cap internationals in support of five hookers – Brian Moore (40 times), John Olver (3) and Mark Regan (12), Richard Cockerill (7) and Andy Long (1).

Leonard developed the natural strength of a junior athlete in discus and javelin, to become the cornerstone of virtually every pack for whom he has played. He started as a 10-year-old and went on to represent Barking, Essex, England Colts, Eastern Counties, England Under 21, Saracens, England B and, from 1990, Harlequins, whom he captained in 1996-97. He scored a try on his Harlequins' debut against Belgium on 15 September 1990 and was in the Quins side who beat Northampton 25–13 in the 1991 Cup final and who were runners-up to Leicester 16–23 in the 1993 final.

He has played in seven Five Nations Championships for England between 1991 and 1997 and it owes something to his power and strength in close quarter operations that England in that time gathered in three Grand Slams and four Triple Crowns. There are those who rated the Leonard-Brian Moore-Jeff Probyn front row as the strongest ever fielded by England. On 14 December 1996, Leonard captained England on their 20–18 Twickenham victory over Argentina and scored his one cap try – a timely score as it turned out.

He was a busy body at the World Cups of 1991 and 1995, being the only forward to play all six games when England were runners-up to Australia in 1991; and playing in five of the six Tests in the 1995 tournament in South Africa, when England lost in the semi-final to New Zealand, 45–29, and lost the third place play-off to France by 19–9.

With the Lions in New Zealand in 1993, Leonard played in eight of the 13 games, being at loose-head against North Auckland, the Maoris (as replacement), Canterbury and Southland and at tight-head against Taranaki, Hawke's Bay and in the second and third Tests, against the All Blacks. In the first Test the Lions' front row comprised Nick Popplewell, Ken Milne and Paul Burnell but for the second and third Tests (the second producing the sole Lions' victory, 20–7) Leonard switched to tight-head to form a front row with Nick Popplewell and Brian Moore.

When the Lions toured South Africa in 1997, Leonard was expected to be the Test tight-head but Paul Wallace (Ireland) was preferred for the fluent style sought by the Lions. Leonard, however, played in seven of the 13 games including as replacement for Tom Smith (Scotland), after seven minutes of the first Test. Leonard thus underlined his considerable value as a prop who can operate on either side of his hooker to equally handsome effect.

1997. Prop on the move – Jason Leonard, ball in hand, against Eastern Province.

ONE NAME ALWAYS LIVES UP TO THE CHALLENGE.

What more could you ask of a major player than endurance, consistency and a world-wide reputation?

Land Rover can offer you all this and more, with Defender giving you a combination of raw strength and practicality which make it the toughest 4x4 around.

If it's all-round performance you're looking for then the Discovery can satisfy all your needs. With the choice of engines and up to seven seats, there's no better vehicle for offering complete versatility.

And nothing has earned itself a reputation as a serious 4x4 player faster than the impressive new Freelander.

To complete this winning team comes the leader of the pack, Range Rover.

And with the added advantages of Freedom Finance and, where status permits, Diplomatic concessions, we can provide the package that takes performance to new heights.

For more information call one of the numbers below.

THE BEST 4x4xFAR

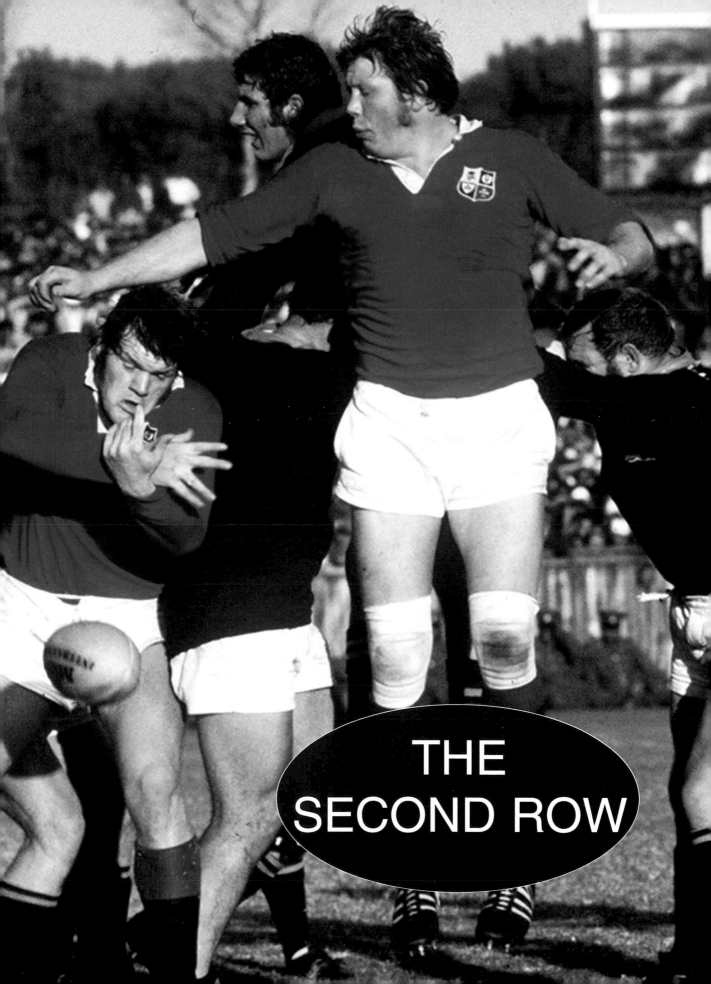

THE
SECOND ROW

W.J. McBRIDE

Ballymena

IRELAND

Born 6 June 1940, Belfast
6ft 3in – 16st 12lbs

63 caps for Ireland
first versus England 1962
last versus Wales 1975

British Lions – 5 tours, 17 Tests
1962 – South Africa (3,4)
1966 – Australia/New Zealand (2,3,4)
1968 – South Africa (1,2,3,4)
1971 – New Zealand (1,2,3,4)
1974 – South Africa (1,2,3,4)

LOCK

Arguably the British Lion commanding most respect from friend and foe alike all over the world has been Willie John McBride, the legendary Irishman, spawned by the Ballymena club. He was a renowned rugby stalwart not only in Ireland's Five Nations Championship triumph in 1974 but as the captain of the British Lions' party who set a new mark in 1974 by completing a tour of South Africa unbeaten, with 21 wins and one draw in their 22 games.

It speaks volumes for the determination and character of Willie John that, even during a spell when Ireland proved disappointingly unsuccessful in Five Nations play except for that 1974 championship, he took on the stature of an exceptional player, with the raw-boned outlines of an All Black and a simple philosophy of total commitment and application, a resolve to meet fire with fire and never to take a backward step. It was mostly attributable to the McBride approach that his famous New Zealand adversary, Colin Meads, once made the rueful

comment that 'those Lions no longer believe in fairies at the bottom of the garden' and that the 1974 Lions in South Africa simply refused to be intimidated.

This mighty man of Ulster took up the rugby union game in his later years at Ballymena Academy and at one time he held the record with Mick Molloy (UC Galway and London Irish) of forming the Irish boilerhouse partnership in 26 cap internationals. He gained his first cap as a 21-year-old against England in 1962 and, within four months, he had been selected for the Lions' tour of South Africa. That was the start of a 21-year association with the Lions, encompassing five tours and a record 17 Tests as a player and the 1983 tour as the manager in New Zealand.

Following the Lions' success in New Zealand in 1971 when he took over the pack leadership after Ray McLoughlin (Ireland) was injured, McBride proved an inspirational figure in the Lions' Test series success and then proclaimed that he 'could now die happy'! The captain of that Lions' tour, John Dawes, described the famous Irish lock as 'a great man, a great forward, a great Lion'. In his book on the tour John Reason wrote that 'Bill McBride went through his fourth Lions tour as a most responsible and effective contributor'. McBride then underlined his quality and his character with another splendid performance when the Barbarians beat the touring All Blacks at Cardiff in arguably the greatest game of them all in January 1973.

When he played for Ireland against England on 16 February 1974, McBride broke the world record of 55 caps held by the mighty Meads and it is only recently that the New Zealand captain, Sean Fitzpatrick, has surpassed Willie John's record of 80 major international appearances. Fitzpatrick has made 92 Test appearances for New Zealand. In his last international game, against Wales at Cardiff on 15 March 1975, McBride was Irish captain again in their centenary season.

McBride could also get up a fair measure of speed for a big man, as he demonstrated against France in April 1967 when he achieved an edge of pace that caught his opponents by surprise to create a try for his boilerhouse partner, Mick Molloy, that brought the house down at Lansdowne Road. It was on the 1968 Lions' tour to South Africa that McBride scored the only Lions' Test try. J.B.G. Thomas wrote: 'J.W. Telfer and W.J. McBride, for most of the tour, rarely were a hundred per cent fit yet played on bravely in proving themselves devoted tourists'. In 1971 and 1974, however, William John McBride reached peaks of leadership, endeavour and courage that marked him out as one from the very top drawer.

The admiration and affection directed towards this giant of the game was never demonstrated to stronger effect than in the delight expressed by the Lansdowne Road crowd when Willie John scored his only cap international try with a typical bullocking run against France in 1975. The vast majority of his contemporaries as players would happily concede that the one colleague they would want to have alongside them when shrapnel was flying would be Willie John. He has since developed into one of the most accomplished public speakers with a natural gift for making his audience sore with laughter at his delightfully uncomplicated anecdotes laced with joyous humour.

1974. Willie John McBride, a big man and a great leader.

W.B. BEAUMONT

Fylde

ENGLAND

Born 9 March 1952, Preston
6ft 3in – 16st 2lbs

34 caps for England
first versus Ireland 1975
last versus Scotland 1982

British Lions – 2 tours, 7 Tests
1977 – New Zealand (2,3,4)
1980 – South Africa (1,2,3,4)

LOCK

It's hard to believe that William Blackledge Beaumont, born in Preston, started his rugby-playing career as a full back at Ellesmere College, because he developed into one of the most effective lock forwards in the history of the English and Lions' rugby game as well as one of the most popular and successful captains. He was a lock without frills, a grafting journeyman forward who would scrummage until the cows came home and who proved eminently reliable as a source of line-out ball as front jumper as well as being possessed of great ball-handling skills and formidable strength.

One high point of Beaumont's lengthy career, which was cut short on medical advice following injuries sustained whilst leading Lancashire in the 1982 County Championship final, was his captaincy of England to their 1980 Grand Slam, their first since 1957. There was none of the bluster or finger-wagging about his leadership but a quiet unassuming approach that created instant rapport with his colleagues. He had other memorable experiences as captain – when the mighty

All Blacks were beaten 21–9 by the North of England at Otley on 17 November 1979, a remarkable four tries to one triumph that created the confidence and focus that later was to lead to Bill Beaumont being carried shoulder-high from the Murrayfield stage on 15 March 1980, after he had inspired England to their 1980 Grand Slam with a 30–18 win over Scotland. He has also made rueful reference to that occasion at Twickenham when he was giving his half-time exhortation to his troops only to find that none of them were listening to him because Erica Roe had entered the arena, to dramatic effect on his players!

Curiously, Beaumont first gained England cap recognition because of injury to Roger Uttley (Gosforth) that led to a hurried request for the Fylde stalwart to join the England party in Dublin for the Ireland game in 1975. It didn't take long for the likeable Lancastrian to create an impression that was to launch him into regular England status and 34 caps in all, the last in the 9–9 draw with Scotland at Murrayfield in January 1982. By then he had captained England a record 21 times and had played with seven different partners in the England stoke room. On 12 occasions he partnered Maurice Colclough (Angoulême, Wasps, Swansea) with whom he also formed a powerful Lions' partnership in South Africa in 1980. Coincidentally it was an injury to his England boilerhouse partner, Nigel Horton (Moseley), that led to Beaumont being called out as replacement to the Lions' tour of New Zealand in 1977 where he formed a formidable engine room partnership with the Scot, Gordon Brown (West of Scotland).

There could have been no more popular choice as captain of the Lions in South Africa in 1980 than Bill Beaumont, the first Englishman to hold that distinction for 50 years, since F.D. Prentice (Leicester) in Australia and New Zealand in 1930.

Sadly the 1980 Lions were dogged by injuries and eight replacement players had to be flown out – so that it was some feat to have won all 14 games outside

the Tests and to have lost three of the four Tests by only 4, 7 and 2 points before winning the fourth in Pretoria by 17–13. Bill Beaumont enhanced his reputation as a leader of men in a highly successful management team with those kenspeckle Irishmen, Syd Millar (manager) and Noel Murphy (assistant manager). The irrepressible Murphy endeared himself to his charges at the first training session when he asked them to 'spread out in a bunch'.

Having served the Fylde club, Lancashire, North of England, England and the Lions with such distinction, Bill Beaumont has become a successful broadcaster as the thoughtful analysis commentator for BBC Television at rugby union internationals. His care and preparation were undoubtedly a factor in his lengthy role as a team captain in the immensely popular *A Question of Sport* television programme. More recently he has become chairman of the RFU's National Playing Committee.

1977.
Above and left
Bill Beaumont wins ball for the Lions against the All Blacks.

P.J. ACKFORD

Plymouth Albion, Rosslyn Park, Metropolitan Police, Harlequins

ENGLAND

LOCK

Born 26 February 1958, West Germany
6ft 6in – 17st 6lbs

22 caps for England
first versus Australia 1988
last versus Australia 1991

British Lions – 1 tour, 3 Tests
1989 – Australia (1,2,3)

Paul John Ackford served a lengthy apprenticeship before gaining cap honours for he first represented England B in 1979 and it was not until nine years later, at the age of 30, that he was first capped against the touring Wallabies at Twickenham in 1988 in England's 28–19 win. He was 33 when he was last capped against the Wallabies at Twickenham in 1991, this time in the final of the World Cup which England lost by 12–6. In that World Cup series he played in five of the six games, missing only that against the USA.

Educated at Plymouth College, the University of Kent and Cambridge University, whom he represented in the 1979 Varsity match, he was a teacher of English literature at Dulwich College and a police inspector in the uniformed branch at Clapham, South West London. Since his retirement from playing he has become one of the most informed and widely read rugby journalists.

Ackford played for Plymouth Albion, Rosslyn Park and the Metropolitan Police and was capped out of the Harlequins' club as a rangy, athletic lock forward with

ball-winning expertise at short throws and good hands. He played for the London Division against Australia in 1981, 1984 and 1988 and it was his outstanding display against them in 1988 that launched him into his cap career. He then proceeded to form a powerful core liaison with Wade Dooley, in 20 cap internationals, a partnership that contributed handsomely to England's 1991 Grand Slam. He represented Devon, Surrey and the South West Division and was a member of London's championship-winning sides of 1988, 1989 and 1990, partly in partnership with his Harlequins Club colleague, Neil Edwards. He first played for Harlequins in September 1987 against Glasgow and was in the cup final teams of 1988 and 1991, both won, and in 1992 when Harlequins lost to Bath, 12–15.

On the Lions' tour of Australia in 1989 Ackford took on a heavy workload – eight of the 12 games – with typical application and big match temperament and played in the three Tests, all bitterly contested. In the successful second and third Tests that brought a Lions' series success for the first time in 15 years he was one of a trio of English police officers, Wade Dooley and Dean Richards (Leicester) being the others, who provided a hard-nosed backbone to the rugged Lions' pack.

Late in the day Ackford might have been in reaching cap status but, once there, he proved a powerful presence and a strong team man who was worth more than his 22 caps.

1989.
Paul Ackford, a commanding presence at the line-outs in Australia.

M.O. JOHNSON

Wigston, Leicester

ENGLAND

Born 9 March 1970, Solihull
6ft 7in – 18st 4lbs

37 caps for England
first versus France 1993
still playing

British Lions – 2 tours, 5 Tests
1993 – New Zealand (2,3)
1997 – South Africa (1,2,3)

LOCK

Martin Osborne Johnson has the distinction of having been chosen to captain the British Lions in South Africa in 1997 without ever having captained his country and having been captain of Leicester on only nine games prior to his Lions' appointment. He also has a special place in rugby legend as captain of the Lions' squad who won the 1997 Test series in South Africa.

It was some guide to the Johnson character that the tour manager, Fran Cotton, said that two important issues in Johnson's appointment had been how he would cope with extreme pressure and 'whether he would operate on the back foot or the front foot'.

New Zealanders don't usually heap praise on English forwards, so that it was a significant accolade for Johnson when, during a playing visit to New Zealand in 1990, he was described by that legendary All Black lock, Colin Meads, as virtually certain to have become an All Black had he stayed down under. Johnson not only played for Meads's King Country in the New Zealand provincial championship but

toured Australia with the New Zealand Colts. However, he returned home in 1991 to make his debut for Leicester in their 1991 Pilkington Cup defeat of Bath.

Johnson was educated at Welland Park and the Robert Smyth Upper School in Market Harborough, joined the Wigston Club as a 12-year-old and became Wigston's first capped player as an eleventh hour replacement for Wade Dooley against France at Twickenham in January 1993. By this time he had graduated through the various grades of the game from England Schools to England A, and later developed into a massive presence on the field with the physical stature to survive in any company, a mighty scrummager and mauler and a sure source of line-out delivery from the number two berth. He has been a vital ingredient in Leicester's successes in recent seasons.

A first choice fixture in the England side since the New Zealand game of 1993, he has played in 31 of the last 35 cap internationals and in the last five, has formed a formidable lock liaison with

Garath Archer of Newcastle. He was the only England forward to play in all six World Cup games in South Africa in 1995. When gaining his 25th cap against Italy at Twickenham on 23 November 1996 he scored his first international try.

When Wade Dooley had to return home from New Zealand in 1993 on the death of his father, Johnson joined the Lions there as a replacement and made such an impression against Taranaki and Auckland as to be chosen as lock partner to Martin Bayfield (Northampton) for the second and third Tests. The second of three brothers, he and brother Will have

occasionally caused some furniture damage at home with their indoor scrummaging practice! Their mother, Hilary, a PE specialist, is a long distance athlete who has competed in London, New York and Paris marathons.

Still, in this professional age, an officer in the Midland Bank, Johnson supports Liverpool Football Club, studies videos of his opponents in action and has created something of a tough guy image: indeed, one renowned rugby correspondent suggested that Johnson with the Lions in South Africa 'might need a script writer but certainly not a bodyguard'.

1997. Martin Johnson, a powerful presence in South Africa.

G.L. BROWN

West of Scotland

SCOTLAND

Born 1 November 1947, Troon
6ft 5in – 16st 12lbs

30 caps for Scotland
first versus South Africa 1969
last versus Ireland 1976

British Lions – 3 tours, 8 Tests
1971 – New Zealand (3,4)
1974 – South Africa (1,2,3)
1977 – New Zealand (2,3,4)

LOCK

It was an unusual statistic of the 1974 Lions' tour to South Africa that sixth in the list of top Lions points-scorers on that tour was that great lump of a Scottish lock forward, Gordon Lamont Brown, who contributed 32 points with eight tries which placed him behind only Tom Grace (St Mary's College and Ireland) and J.J. Williams (Llanelli and Wales) in the top tries list. It was a remarkable achievement by the West of Scotland lock forward, a record for a forward on tour in South Africa, and two of those tries contributed to Lions' victories in the second and third Tests. He already had been involved in the 1971 Lions' tour of New Zealand in which he played in the third and fourth Tests that clinched the series success and he was to tour New Zealand with the Lions again in 1977 when he played in three of the four Tests.

Known affectionately as 'Broon frae Troon', he was a former pupil of Marr College in Troon. Brown had the build of a bison, revelled in scrummaging and was an artful specialist in all the line-out

roles and ruses, developing during the 1974 tour the same resolve to meet fire with fire as demonstrated by his captain and boilerhouse partner, Willie John McBride. Son of Jock Brown, the former Clyde and Scotland goalkeeper, Gordon is the younger brother of Peter Brown (27 caps, 10 times captain of Scotland). It is one of the game's unusual records that during the Wales versus Scotland game in Cardiff in 1970, Gordon had to go on as replacement for his injured brother. A veritable giant in the club game, he was sometimes accused of only reaching one hundred per cent fitness when training daily with the Lions. Yet when he played his last international against Ireland in Dublin in 1976, the 15–6 margin representing Scotland's first win at Lansdowne Road for 10 years, he was second in Scotland's list of most capped locks with 30 to Alastair McHarg's 32.

Although they made an unlikely pairing, Brown the workhorse, McHarg in his amalgam of tight and very loose play, they yet formed Scotland's stokeroom on

a record 22 occasions and so contributed to what many regarded as the strongest-ever Scottish packs during a period in the seventies when Scotland, under the guidance of the inimitable Bill Dickinson of Jordanhill College, enjoyed one of their most successful spells.

Apart from his three Lions' tours, Gordon Brown also toured with Scotland in Argentina 1969 and Australia in 1970. It was in December 1976 that Brown, playing for Glasgow against North and Midlands in the inter-district championship at Murrayfield, was involved in a foul play sequence with Alan Hardie (Gordonians) that resulted in both being sent off. There was some sympathy for Brown whose action had been of a retaliatory nature, but he was suspended for 12 weeks, Hardie for 16 months. As a consequence Brown missed all four games in the 1977 Five Nations Championship, his cap career over, although he had some consolation in the faith the Lions' selectors showed in him by his selection for the 1977 tour of New Zealand.

'Broon frae Troon' led the Lions' choir on that tour, just one of his many accomplishments that have marked him out as fit to stand alongside the greats of the engine-room.

1974. *Above* Gordon Brown, with a little help from his fellow forwards, provides tidy ball for Gareth Edwards against South Africa and (*left*) the powerful second-row combination of Brown and McBride which was at the heart of the Lions' success.

M.J. COLCLOUGH

Angoulême, Wasps, Swansea

ENGLAND

Born 2 September 1953, Oxford
6ft 5in – 17st 10lbs

25 caps for England
first versus Scotland 1978
last versus France 1986

British Lions – 2 tours, 8 Tests
1980 – South Africa (1,2,3,4)
1983 – New Zealand (1,2,3,4)

LOCK

When in 1980 England won their first Grand Slam for 23 years, one of the most important ingredients was the lock forward partnership between the captain, Bill Beaumont, and his extremely large partner, Maurice John Colclough, who turned the scale at nearly 18 stone. They were a super blend, each a scrummaging horse and a formidable mauler and Colclough with the physical wherewithal to stand the buffeting as middle jumper with Beaumont comfortably effective at number two. They were partners, notably, in three of the games in England's 1980 Grand Slam.

Colclough was educated at the Duke of York's RMS in Dover and at Liverpool University, played for Kent and London Schools and for Sussex in 1972 and Lancashire in 1974. After university he moved to Angoulême in France as manager of a leisure centre but took the frequent travel back to England for squad sessions in his stride. Following the regional championship games in 1970 he gained his first cap against Scotland in 1978 and had four

boilerhouse partners during his 25-cap reign – Beaumont for 12 games, John Sydall (Waterloo) for one, Steve Bainbridge (Gosforth and Fylde) for eight and Wade Dooley (Preston Grasshoppers and Fylde) for four.

Colclough captained London Division against Australia 1981 and 1984 and New Zealand 1983 and toured with England in the Far East in 1979 and in North America in 1982. He had the satisfaction of scoring England's try in their 15–9 defeat of the All Blacks at Twickenham in 1983 and, in his last international against Ireland in 1986, he took over the captaincy when Nigel Melville (Wasps) was injured.

On the Lions' tour of South Africa in 1980 he made such an impression in the early games, notably against the Orange Free State, as to force his way into the Test team alongside his England partner Beaumont. Colclough was big enough and rough enough to look the unceremonious Springboks' forwards straight in the eye. He returned home with an enhanced reputation having played in 11 of the 18 tour games and scored one of the Lions' two tries (the other was by Jeff Squire of Wales) in their splendid 16–9 win over the formidable 'Blue Bulls' of Northern Transvaal, captained by Naas Botha.

Three years later the bearded Colclough played in 11 of the 18 games on the Lions' tour of New Zealand, a disastrous tour in that all four Tests were lost, but he figured in the defeats of Bay of Plenty, Wellington, Manawatu, Southland and Waikato and was Lions' captain in the victory over Mid-Canterbury.

Colclough had been fortunate to make the tour because, in England's game against France, he suffered serious knee damage that required lengthy and intensive treatment. He was belatedly passed fit to tour New Zealand, much to the satisfaction of the tour manager, Willie John McBride. It was generally agreed that Colclough, adapting effectively to the front jump position, was the forward success of that disappointing invasion of the land of the long white cloud.

1980. Maurice Colclough battles to get a hand on the ball in a line-out against Transvaal.

W.A. DOOLEY

Preston Grasshoppers, Fylde

ENGLAND

Born 2 October 1957, Warrington
6ft 8in – 17st 10lbs

55 caps for England
first versus Romania 1985
last versus Ireland 1993

British Lions – 2 tours, 2 Tests
1989 – Australia (2,3)
1993 – New Zealand

LOCK

Wade Anthony Dooley is England's most capped lock forward with 55 and lies seventh in the list of the most capped Englishmen behind Rory Underwood (85), Will Carling (72), Rob Andrew (71), Brian Moore (64) Jason Leonard (63) and Peter Winterbottom (58).

Having played rugby league at school, the Beaumont Secondary Technical School in Warrington, where he was born, he took up rugby union when a police cadet and was a Blackpool community police officer during his lengthy career as an England lock.

Dooley first made an impression in representative play as a replacement during the Northern Division's 22–15 win over the touring Romanians at Birkenhead in December 1984 and was first capped as the tallest player ever to represent England (at six feet eight inches) against the same Romanians at Twickenham on 5 January 1985. He played in 55 of the next 63 internationals as the control tower of the England pack alongside six different lock partners – John Orwin (Gloucester) for 13 games,

Steve Bainbridge (Gosforth) for four, Maurice Colclough (Angoulême, Wasps, Swansea) for four, Nigel Redman (Bath) for five, Paul Ackford (Harlequins) for 20, and Martin Bayfield (Northampton) for nine. His mighty scrummaging and midline ball-winning were key factors when England carried all before them in consecutive Grand Slams in 1991 and 1992. He also scored three tries for England – against France in 1986, USA in 1987 (World Cup) and Wales in 1992.

Dooley's success proved something of an incentive for players in clubs outside the top echelon, in that he proved that membership of a slightly lower grade club need be no bar to cap achievement. Almost all his club service was with Preston Grasshoppers. When first capped, his club were lying seventh in the Northern Division qualifying table with just three wins from 10 games. At the end of his international career Preston Grasshoppers were lying third in National League Division 4 North.

With Finlay Calder's Lions in Australia in 1989, Dooley played in seven of the 12 games, all seven won. After the Lions had played second fiddle at the line-outs in the first Test, which they lost by 12–30, Dooley was introduced to perform alongside his England partner Paul Ackford and proved the ideal, hard-nosed citizen for the unceremonious and, at times, bitter, exchanges. Partly through Dooley's display the Lions won 19–12. In the third Test, which the Lions won 19–18, he made another powerful contribution to the first series win for 15 years. Although not quite in the Gordon Brown class of 1974, Dooley also weighed in with tries against Queensland B and the Australian Capital Territories.

He also toured with the Lions in New Zealand in 1993 but after playing against North Auckland, New Zealand Maoris and Otago, he had to return home on the death of his father. His power and experience were much missed even though his replacement, Martin Johnson, did make the Test side. Throughout his career Wade Dooley proved to be not only a big man in stature but in giving his all for club, division and country.

1989. Wade Dooley retains possession for the Lions in the game against ACT.

LOCK

J.W. DAVIDSON

Dungannon, London Irish

IRELAND

Born 28 April 1974, Belfast
6ft 6in – 18st

12 caps for Ireland
first versus Fiji 1995
still playing

British Lions – 1 tour, 3 Tests
1997 – South Africa (1,2,3)

LOCK

In the wake of the mighty series-winning achievement by the 1997 Lions in South Africa, many of the pundits were agreed that the most improved player was Jeremy William Davidson, the towering Irish lock, who lived up to the pre-tour prophecy about him by former Lions' captain John Dawes that he would provide 'the fire and brimstone so typical of the Irish and much needed in South Africa'. Davidson did more than that. Not only did he have to overcome natural nervousness at training and playing with players who already had star status, he also had to adapt to a style of rugby in South Africa that was more physical than anything he had experienced before as well as being faster and more fluent than that of the Five Nations Championship. He rose to the occasion so impressively that his Lions' predecessor as a lock, Paul Ackford, wrote that 'men like Lawrence Dallaglio and Jeremy Davidson are fast becoming the complete rugby player. They are confident in all phases, equally happy popping up outside a speeding Scott

Gibbs as they are grovelling for possession at the bottom of a maul'.

Davidson had played in the final of the Ulster Schools Cup and for the Irish Schools in a 9–15 defeat by England Schools at Bedford, both in 1992. Out of Methodist College, Belfast, he went on the Irish Schools' tour to New Zealand in the summer of 1992, played in the Ireland Under 21 side which beat England Under 21 in 1994 and, in December of that year, made his Ulster debut. He toured with Ireland in Australia in 1994, played in four of the eight games and scored a try against Western Australia.

Although performing as a lock forward it was as a blind side flanker that he gained his third cap in the 44–8 win over Fiji at Lansdowne Road on 18 November 1995. Indeed his first three cap internationals were as a flanker, since when he has played nine in a row as a lock forward. He made such an impression as to have been in 12 of 13 cap internationals between Fiji in 1995 and Scotland in 1997, missing only the match against the USA in January 1996 because of injury. He had missed much of 1994-95 because of a back injury.

His versatility was probably a factor in his selection for the 1997 Lions' tour to South Africa but it was generally believed that he would be more of a mid-week than a Test player. The Irishman, however, had no intention of aiming just at the mid-week selection and, although he might have had to battle strongly for a Test berth if Scotland's Doddie Weir had not been so grievously injured, Davidson made such an impression as to gain the Test spot in preference to England's Simon Shaw. He played in eight of the 13 games including all three Tests and was described as having 'caught everything thrown at him as well as competing energetically in the loose'. He also adapted very well to the throwing-in of three different hookers and continued to compete with dogged determination, even though the South Africans clearly had him marked out as a danger – twice in the second Test he had his legs taken away in mid-air.

Davidson was described by Rob Andrew as one of those deserving of special mention for the advance made during the tour and the Dungannon and London Irish lock also was given special praise for 'winning the line-out of his life from which stemmed Jeremy Guscott's series-clinching drop goal'. With all he has learned with the Lions, Davidson should be a strong man in Irish ranks for years to come although it was heart-breaking that injury ruled him out of the entire 1998 Five Nations Championship, during which he gained experience as a television pundit.

1997. Jeremy Davidson rises above the South Africans to win vital line-out ball for the Lions during the second Test at Durban.

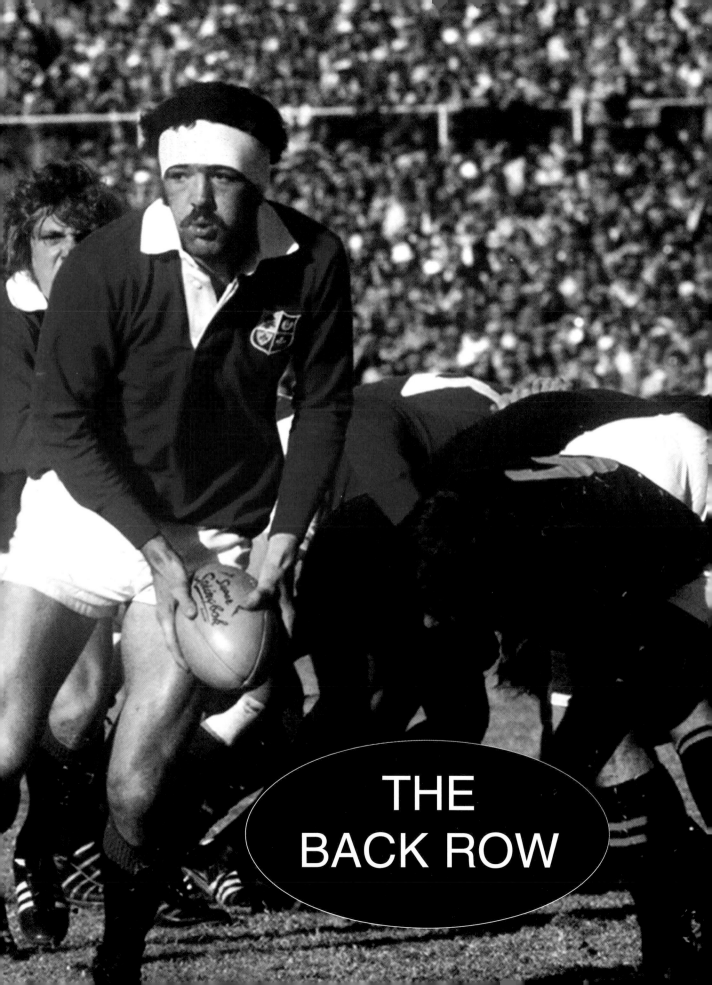

THE
BACK ROW

P.J. DIXON

Harlequins, Gosforth

ENGLAND

Born 30 April 1944, Keighley
6ft 3in – 15st 1lb

22 caps for England
first versus The President's XV 1971
last versus New Zealand 1978

British Lions – 1 tour, 3 Tests
1971 – Australia/New Zealand (1,2,4)

It is unusual for a player to be selected for the British Lions before he has played for his country but that is the distinction achieved by Peter John Dixon – a strong, driving, non-stop flank forward and no slouch about the paddock, who seemed to be out of a New Zealand mould with a nose for ball and action points. It was only after he was chosen for the Lions' tour to Australia and New Zealand in 1971 that he gained his first cap out of the Harlequins' club against The President's Overseas XV on 17 April 1971, to celebrate the centenary of the Rugby Football Union. On that day the opposing breakaway trio comprised Ian Kirkpatrick, Brian Lochore (both New Zealand) and Greg Davis (Australia) but Dixon, capped as a 27-year-old, held his own and put the experience to good use.

Educated at St Bees in Cumberland (out of which he played for England Schools) Dixon attended the University of Durham, played for Workington and the UAU and gained four Blues at Oxford University in 1967, 1968, 1969 and 1970. He had considerable influence on those Varsity games, scoring a try in 1968 and, following the shock Oxford win by 14–3 in 1970, being described thus by Gordon Ross in *Playfair Rugby Annual*:'It is perhaps invidious to single out one from so effective a pack but if one does then Dixon is the man.' Dixon was described by one of his Oxford colleagues as 'one of the best thinking players in the game'. It was not surprising, therefore, when he captained England against France in Paris on 26 February 1972 and against Scotland at Murrayfield three weeks later.

Dixon joined Gosforth in 1972 and formed a formidable breakaway unit there with Roger Uttley and David Robinson, playing in the John Player Cup finals against Rosslyn Park in 1976 and against Waterloo a year later. Gosforth won both finals, to underline their high status in the England club game and their 'loosies' proved a key element. Dixon was also a loyal stalwart for Cumberland-Westmoreland in the county championship.

BLIND SIDE

It was thoroughly disappointing for Dixon who had so much to offer that during his Five Nations spell between 1972 and 1978 England suffered some heavy defeats, failed to gather in an outright championship and gained only the shared quintuple tie in 1973 when all five countries won twice at home and lost twice away. That series, however, brought one of Dixon's finest performances when he scored two tries in England's 20–13 defeat of Scotland at Twickenham on 17 March 1973 which deprived the Scots of a Triple Crown. It was instinctive support running, a Dixon hallmark, that brought his first try. The second was the result of a perfect line-out tail peel, Andy Ripley tapping down, Fran Cotton rumbling round the tail and Dixon at Tony Neary's elbow to score. That breakaway trio of Dixon, Ripley and Neary were regarded as one of the best ever fielded by England. They played together in a record 12 cap internationals in a row.

Dixon once made a round trip of 24,000 miles for just one game. He was one of five replacement players flown out to join England's tour party in Australia in 1975 and just had time for one game, the last against Queensland Country.

Having been unavailable for England's tour to South Africa in 1972 Dixon was unlucky to miss out on seven games against Southern Hemisphere giants – four versus Australia, two versus New Zealand and one versus South Africa – and the only such game in which he took part was against the All Blacks at Twickenham on 25 November 1978, when he formed the loose forward combine with Roger Uttley and Mike Rafter. That was Dixon's last cap, at the age of 34. He scored four tries in cap internationals – two against Scotland in 1973 and others against France in 1976 (when he was described as England's best forward) and Ireland in 1978.

Dixon already had stated his credentials on the Lions' 1971 tour of

1971. Peter Dixon (right) and Mervyn Davies watch as Gareth Edwards gets the ball away during the second Test at Christchurch.

Australia and New Zealand when he played in 15 of the 26 games and in three of the four Tests, by which the Lions became the first to win a full series in New Zealand. Dixon and Derek Quinnell (Wales) brilliantly neutralised the threat posed by Syd Going, the New Zealand scrum half, especially in blind side darts. Dixon also formed a very effective breakaway blend with Mervyn Davies (Wales) and John Taylor (Wales) and scored a typical support try towards their 14–14 draw in the fourth Test that clinched the series. Carwyn James, the legendary Lions' coach, appreciated in full the Dixon contribution: 'Peter really does know the game. When things go wrong in training or he thinks something is wrong round the back of the scrum, he is usually first to spot it. He is usually right too and is not afraid to speak up.' Praise indeed from the master coach.

BLIND SIDE

R.M. UTTLEY

Gosforth, Wasps

ENGLAND

Born 11 September 1949, Blackpool
6ft 4in – 15st 10lbs

23 caps for England
first versus Ireland 1973
last versus Scotland 1980

British Lions – 1 tour, 4 Tests
1974 – South Africa (1,2,3,4)

BLIND SIDE

When Roger Miles Uttley joined Peter Dixon as the only two Gosforth club players to be capped at that time, the circumstances were unusual. The occasion was the Irish match in Dublin on 10 February 1973. Political troubles had forced Scotland and Wales to cancel visits to Dublin in 1972 so when John Pullin's England side took the field at Lansdowne Road a year later, they were accorded a lengthy standing ovation by the 50,000 crowd. Uttley and Steve Smith (Sale) were the only new caps. What a baptism – especially as Ireland won 18–9.

On that occasion Uttley was at lock forward, a position he took in his first 11 cap assignments before being converted into a loose forward on the Lions' tour to South Africa in 1974. One of the most versatile back five forwards ever to play for England, Uttley's 23 caps comprised 11 as lock, seven as number eight and five as flanker. He would have had many more but for a broken leg in January 1976 and recurring back trouble that caused him to withdraw from the Lions' tour to New Zealand in 1977 which many thought he should have captained.

Having been educated at Blackpool Grammar School and Northumberland College of Education, from which he graduated as a schoolmaster, Uttley spent most of his senior career with Gosforth and Northumberland but moved to Wasps in 1979 when he became a member of staff at Harrow School. At Gosforth he formed a very effective loose forward alliance with Peter Dixon and David Robinson: they were his flankers when he captained Gosforth from number eight to the club's John Player Cup final win by 27–11 over Waterloo at Twickenham on 16 April 1977. Uttley missed part of the first half to have six stitches inserted in a cut right ear but returned to join Dixon and Robinson in a whole series of rolling moves off rucks and mauls that sapped Waterloo's strength.

Uttley had toured with England in Japan and the Far East in 1971 before gaining his first cap and taking part in that remarkable England tour of New Zealand in August and September 1973. All three provincial games were lost, yet England won the Test against the All Blacks by 16–10 in Auckland. Uttley locked the scrummage with Chris Ralston (Richmond), as he was to do on 10 cap international occasions. Actually the only home season during which Uttley played as an international flanker was 1979-80 when he played a strong role, especially in tackle, harassment and line-out supply, in England's first Grand Slam win for 23 years.

Uttley captained England on five occasions – in the 1977 Five Nations and against Scotland in 1979. His two cap international tries were scored against Australia in Brisbane on 31 May 1975 and in the 26–6 defeat of Scotland at Twickenham on 8 January 1977 when, as number eight, he thundered over from a close range scrummage. In that Brisbane Test he played as wing forward having performed in the first Test in Sydney a week earlier as a lock.

His range of ability had already been demonstrated on the Lions' 1974 tour when he had a heavy workload of 16 games out of the 22, yet never slackened his workrate. He featured eight times as lock, once as number eight (scoring a try against Southern Universities) and seven as wing forward (flanker), four of these in the Test matches. As a blind side flanker Uttley performed brilliantly the function that his Gosforth colleague Dixon and Derek Quinnell had achieved in New Zealand in 1971, by virtually closing up the narrow side and thus reducing South African options. Uttley was a key member of arguably the strongest pack ever fielded by the Lions – Ian McLauchlan, Bobby Windsor, Fran Cotton, Gordon Brown, Willie John McBride, Uttley, Mervyn Davies and Fergus Slattery. They were at the heart of the Lions' victory in the Test series, the first time the South Africans had lost a home series this century. Typical Uttley tenacity led to the opening Lions' try in the crucial fourth Test – pressure on the South African scrum half, a loose pass and Uttley's pounce to score. As one tour report said: 'Uttley was chosen for the tour as a lock but was a huge success as a wing forward.'

A few months after the South African safari Uttley was reunited with his Test colleagues Mervyn Davies and Fergus Slattery in the Barbarians' side who held the touring All Blacks to a 13–13 draw at Twickenham on 30 November 1974.

It was a measure of the respect in which he was held that in 1989 Uttley joined Ian McGeechan as coach to the Lions in Australia, a tour in which the Lions' forwards, coached by Uttley, more than held their own against a tough hard Australian pack. Uttley played his part in forging a strong team spirit that helped win the series. He has now taken on the role of England team manager, having in the past been the England forwards' coach.

1974.
A tattered Roger Uttley in the thick of things against the South Africans.

M.C. TEAGUE

Gloucester, Cardiff, Stroud, Moseley

ENGLAND

Born 8 October 1960, Gloucester
6ft 3in – 16st 7lbs

27 caps for England
first versus France 1985 (R)
last versus Ireland 1993

British Lions – 2 tours, 3 Tests
1989 – Australia (2,3)
1993 – New Zealand (2)

The nickname 'Iron Mike' was given to the world heavyweight champion Mike Tyson, but to the rugby folk of the south west of England the man who deserved the title more was Michael Clive Teague, a rugged, strong man loose forward who made quite an impact on the English game between 1987 and 1993. Notably he was given the accolade 'Player of the Series' when the Lions gained Test series success in Australia in 1989.

As a self-employed builder he was naturally strong and he allied this physical hardness to typical West Country commitment and aggression and wholehearted application, not least to the less glamorous chores. His stirring example proved inspirational to his colleagues especially when the 1989 Lions were in Australia and there was a particular need for a tough, uncompromising stance by the Lions' forwards against hard rivals.

Born in Gloucester and educated at the Churchtown School there, he played first for the All Blues Club in Gloucester, then for Oxleaze, Gloucester first in 1979,

Cardiff, Stroud and Moseley. He represented Gloucester in the cup finals of 1982, when the only drawn final resulted in a cup share between Gloucester and Moseley, and in 1990 when Bath were the winners.

In 1991 he played for England B against France B but it wasn't until 1985 that he entered the list of cap players when he replaced Bath's John Hall after 55 minutes of the French game. There followed an intermittent international career when he missed the next three cap internationals, played number eight in the two Tests on the tour of New Zealand of 1985 (scoring a try in the first at Christchurch), then missing out in the next 21 games partly through injury, until the Scotland match in 1989.

Teague made an impressive contribution to England's 1991 Grand Slam as blind side flanker, scoring tries against Wales in Cardiff and Ireland in Dublin. His was the only try in that Cardiff international when England won by 25–6, their first triumph there for 28 years. It was no great surprise that that try stemmed from a scrummage drive, for he was a pick-up artiste par excellence. He had sound technique and determination as well as a strong, low body position in the drive as time and again committing opponents over the gain line and so providing more fertile conditions for his backs to prosper.

A versatile type, Teague gained 19 caps as blind side flanker and eight as number eight, but he was also adept at providing line-out support and protection for his specialists.

In the 1991 World Cup he played in five of the six games, being rested for the USA match. He was blind side flanker in partnership with Dean Richards (Leicester) and Peter Winterbottom (Harlequins) against New Zealand and Italy but switched to number eight with Michael Skinner (Harlequins) and Winterbottom as his flankers against France and Scotland and in the 12–6 defeat by Australia in the final.

Teague'. He played against Western Australia, Queensland, New South Wales, in the second and third Tests and against the Anzac XV, all won. He was injured before the first Test which the Lions lost 12–30 but when Teague was introduced to partner the captain Finlay Calder and Richards in the breakaway unit, he set a splendid example of controlled aggression that was a big factor in the Lions' Test victories by 19–12 and 19–18.

Although he did not figure large in the Tests of the Lions' tour to New Zealand in 1993, Ben Clarke (Bath), Richards and Winterbottom forming the breakaway unit in all three, Teague had a busy schedule in eight of the 13 games, scoring a try in the 49–25 defeat of Taranaki and appearing as replacement in the second Test when he temporarily took over for Winterbottom.

1989. Mike Teague, the Lions' man of the series in Australia.

Undoubtedly a high point of his career was his magnificent form for the 1989 Lions in Australia. One report pointed to 'the Lions' pack having developed very well based partly on the brilliance of Paul Ackford, Dean Richards and Mike

Mike Teague deserved more than his 27 caps spread over nine seasons but whenever he was called upon he gave his all, to most notable effect against the Wallabies: all his opponents, however, saw him as 'Iron Mike' indeed.

L.B.N. DALLAGLIO

Wasps

ENGLAND

Born 10 August 1972, London
6ft 4in – 16st 7lbs

20 caps for England
first versus South Africa 1995 (R)
still playing

British Lions – 1 tour, 3 Tests
1997 – South Africa (1,2,3)

BLIND SIDE

The seven-a-side game has been responsible on more than one occasion for launching a young player on to the international stage and towards future stardom: this can certainly be said of Lawrence Bruno Nero Dallaglio, of Italian stock, who first made an impact in England's side who won the World Sevens tournament at Murrayfield in April 1993 by beating Australia in the final by 21–17.

Dallaglio, then 21, showed the ball sense, skill levels and judgment of what subsequently had him marked out as the complete loose forward, for he also underlined his tackle qualities in the one-to-one situations for which the short game is renowned. Since then he has become an integral part of England's breakaway trio and already has captained England in eight cap internationals.

He was educated at Ampleforth College and Kingston University and demonstrated his potential early on by representing England at virtually every level – Schools 18 Group, Colts (three games), Under 21 (five), Emergent XV,

Students and A. He gained his first cap in the 14–24 Twickenham defeat by the Springboks on 18 November 1995 when he replaced the injured Tim Rodber after 66 minutes. He would have played 15 cap internationals in a row but missed the 1997 Welsh match because of flu and, of course, missed the 1997 caps tour to Argentina because he was on Lions duty.

Dallaglio is another wonderfully versatile forward who played lock for England against the Orange Free State in the 1994 tour to South Africa and was then asked to play as open side flanker by Jack Rowell because of his developing football skills. However, the general feeling is that his most effective position is blind side flanker where he has operated in 13 of his 20 cap games and where he showed outstanding form on six occasions for the Lions in South Africa. Tall enough at six feet four inches and athletic enough to prove a dependable line-out auxiliary purveyor, he is also pretty quick for such a big man so that his tackling carries vigorous impact. The RFU Player of the Season in 1995-96, he has scored five cap international tries – against Western Samoa at Twickenham on 16 December 1995 (he also scored for London and the South East against the Samoans), against Italy at Twickenham on 23 November 1996 (all three English 'looses' scored tries, the others being Tim Rodber and Chris Sheasby), against France at Twickenham on 1 March 1997 when he showed pace, power and judgment and against both New Zealand and Wales on 6 December 1997 and 21 February 1998 respectively.

He has revelled in the attractive style of play adopted by Wasps, whom he has captained during the past two seasons, having been in their side in the Pilkington Cup final against Bath on 6 May 1995. When Wasps lost Rob Andrew, Steve Bates and Dean Ryan to Newcastle, Dallaglio made such an imprint as captain that Wasps have flourished as Courage League champions in the 1996-97 season.

Dallaglio has suffered two main disappointments – being overlooked for the 1995 World Cup in South Africa and being strongly tipped for the English captaincy which, instead, fell to Bath's Philip de Glanville in 1997. Yet it was typical of Dallaglio that he gave total support to the captain, not least when, having just played in the final Test for the Lions in South Africa, he dashed off to Sydney there to lead England's pack against the Wallabies one week later. He then took over the England captaincy against Australia at Twickenham in the 15–15 draw on 15 November 1997.

Having played against Orange Free State and South Africa A and Eastern Province (the last two as flanker) during England's tour to South Africa in 1994, Dallaglio was just the type to meet the South Africans head on with the Lions in 1997 when he played in seven of the 13 games including all three Tests. He also scored a try in the outstanding 42–12 win over Natal.

It was hardly surprising that in the first two Tests which the Lions won they fielded arguably one of the best England loose forward combinations ever – Dallaglio, Tim Rodber (number eight) and Richard Hill. Dallaglio was a big success on tour. However, he will lose the England captaincy as he is unavailable for England's 1998 summer tour of the Southern Hemisphere because of a long-term shoulder injury.

1997. Lawrence Dallaglio breaks through the tackle of Springbok Danie van Schalkwyk in the third Test at Ellis Park.

J. TAYLOR

London Welsh

WALES

Born 21 July 1945, Watford
5ft 11in – 13st 9lbs

26 caps for Wales
first versus Scotland 1967
last versus France 1973

British Lions – 2 tours, 4 Tests
1968 – South Africa
1971 – Australia/New Zealand (1,2,3,4)

OPEN SIDE

The Welsh selectors took something of a gamble when they launched John Taylor of London Welsh into his caps career against Scotland at Murrayfield in 1967, for he was one of six new caps and had rocketed up the ratings on the basis of a national trial appearance following just four senior club games. He proved to be an inspired choice, however, for Taylor developed into the complete open side wing forward, blessed with impressive pace, safe hands, unfettered commitment to the tackle and an instinctive sense of productive positioning. He could kick goals too. Perhaps in the modern game he might be regarded as just too small – he used to experience some annoyance when a certain Scottish commentator used to refer to him as 'wee John Taylor' – but he was such a gifted all-round footballer as to have been able to make an impression in any era.

His skill levels were underlined when he was a member of the Loughborough Colleges side who beat Northampton 29–10 in the 1966 Middlesex final. He graduated as a schoolmaster from Loughborough, having attended Watford

Grammar School and gained his Welsh qualification from his mother. He joined London Welsh in 1966 during his last year at Loughborough and within a year he had gained a cap and, not so long after that, he was chosen for the Lions.

Known to his cronies as 'Basil Brush' he perhaps will be remembered most for his majestic touch line conversion of the Gerald Davies try that clinched Wales's 19–18 victory over Scotland at Murrayfield in 1971. That led to a Welsh Grand Slam and was rated as 'the greatest conversion since Saint Paul'.

Taylor shared in the remarkable success of London Welsh when they set impressive standards of fluent, total rugby during the late sixties and seventies. He captained the club to two consecutive Middlesex Sevens finals in 1973 and 1974, and struck up a liaison at Old Deer Park with Mervyn Davies that led to notable success with Wales and the Lions. He also had a keen rival for the national open-side berth, his London Welsh club mate, Tony Gray. Taylor captained London Welsh in his last

row. Taylor and David Morris of Neath were the Welsh wing forwards in 22 cap internationals and, with Mervyn Davies, they created arguably the finest loose forward trio ever fielded by Wales. They formed a breakaway unit on 18 occasions and supplied a superb amalgam of overall speed, ball winning, ball usage, linkage with their backs and uncanny anticipation that proved vital ingredients in the Welsh Triple Crown and championship in 1969 and their Grand Slam in 1971.

Taylor toured with Wales in Australasia in 1969, played in four of the seven games, three of them internationals against New Zealand, Australia and Fiji and scored three of his seven international tries there – one against the Wallabies and two against Fiji in a non-cap match. His other cap tries were against Scotland in 1971 and 1972, Ireland 1969 and The President's XV in 1970. He also potted three conversions and two penalty goals in cap internationals.

South Africa 1968 was not a happy hunting ground for Taylor, who was dogged by injury and played in only five of the 20 games. But the 1971 Lions played the kind of open, handling rugby that was meat and drink to a roving, skilful forward like Taylor. Swift and constructive, he was a big success, playing in 15 of the 26 games (14 of which were won), scoring tries against Counties-Thames Valley, Wellington, Otago and Southland and playing in all four Tests with his London Welsh mate Mervyn Davies. In the third Test Taylor made a typical crushing tackle on New Zealand full back Laurie Mains that led to a Barry John drop goal, snaffled two New Zealand throws at the line-out and was described as having a 'magnificent game in defence'. One tour report said: 'John Taylor proved an extremely capable player and as the open side, the quickest of the loosies, that enabled him to spin across field in a moving defensive wall. In a way a man for all seasons.'

1971.
John Taylor at Barry John's elbow in the final Test at Auckland to provide support if required.

OPEN SIDE

season 1977-78 and even so late in his career, at 32, he still displayed his static strength for staying on his feet and his aggressive defence and cover.

When he toured South Africa with the 1968 Lions, Taylor was so appalled at the effect of the apartheid system there that when the South Africans toured the UK in 1969-70 he informed the Welsh selectors that he did not wish to be considered for the international against them. He also missed out on the 1970 matches against Scotland, England and Ireland but was restored for the French match and played in the next 12 Five Nations matches in a

J.F. SLATTERY

UCD, Blackrock College

IRELAND

Born 12 February 1949, Dublin
6ft 1in – 14st 9lbs

61 caps for Ireland
first versus South Africa 1970
last versus France 1984

British Lions – 2 tours, 4 Tests
1971 – Australia/New Zealand
1974 – South Africa (1,2,3,4)

OPEN SIDE

Of all the attacking flank forwards who have come out of Ireland, among them Noel Murphy, Ronnie Kavanagh, Jim McCarthy, Bill McKay, John O'Driscoll and Stewart McKinney, the name of John Fergus Slattery surely would be strongly in contention for selection to any World XV – for not only does he still hold the world record for a flanker of 61 caps but he was an automatic choice for Irish teams during 14 seasons of Five Nations Championship rugby.

In that lengthy career he never departed from an all-action, dynamic style that marked him out as special. His pace about the paddock and to the break down, his ferocious tackling and his fitness, hardness and ball winning capability made him highly respected and feared. Sundry stand-off halves have had their confidence and rhythm ruined by that hunting-dog-type hounding of a Slattery who saw it as a main part of his function to disrupt opposing moves by placing instant pressure upon their ball carrier, be he back or forward.

He became an estate agent after attending Blackrock College and University College, both in Dublin, and remained loyal to Blackrock throughout his career.

He was still a student at University College, Dublin when first capped against Dawie de Villiers' Springboks at Lansdowne Road on 10 January 1970. The South Africans won a huge share of possession but were held to an 8–8 draw, this reflecting immense credit on Ron Lamont (Instonians), Slattery and Ken Goodall (City of Derry) for their part in keeping the door closed. Thereafter Slattery played against France (15 times), England and Scotland (12 each), Wales (11), Australia (4), New Zealand and South Africa (3 each), missed six games through injury in 1976 and 1977 and played his last 33 cap internationals in a row. He formed arguably Ireland's most effective breakaway unit with John O'Driscoll (London Irish and Manchester) and his Blackrock clubmate, Willie Duggan. They played 20 cap internationals together and were a vital element in Ireland's championship and

Triple Crown success in 1982 and their shared championship with France in 1983.

Slattery's inspirational and tactical strengths also were outlined in his captaincy of Ireland in 17 consecutive cap internationals from the French match of 1979 up to and including the Australian game in 1981. He was succeeded by Ciaran Fitzgerald (St Mary's College). Slattery captained Ireland on their tour of Australia in 1979 when he played in all eight games, including the victories over the Wallabies by 27–12 and 9–3. The Irish lost only one game – to Sydney by only 12–16. In South Africa 1981 he was captain again, played five of the seven games and reached the milestone of his 50th cap in the first Test in Cape Town. Reports referred to the prodigious work rate of Slattery, Duggan and O'Driscoll, Slattery scoring three tries in the match against the South African President's Trophy XV.

He played three times for the Barbarians against major touring sides and never experienced defeat. He scored a try and linked brilliantly for one by J.P.R. Williams in that famous 23–11 win over the All Blacks at Cardiff on 27 January 1973; he also played in the 13–13 draw with the All Blacks at Twickenham on 30 November 1974 and the 19–7 win over the Wallabies at Cardiff on the 24 January 1976.

It seemed in every sense appropriate that he should be part of arguably the most successful Lions' tours of all time – 1971 in Australia and New Zealand when he played in 13 of the 26 games, being deprived of a third Test place by a throat infection so that John Taylor (Wales) played in all four Tests. Those Lions lost only two of 26 games, to Queensland and the second Test. Three years later in South Africa, Slattery played in 12 of 22 games, scored six tries and formed the loose forward trio in all four Tests with Mervyn Davies (Wales) and Roger Uttley (England). Slattery also had a late try disallowed in the final Test that would have given the Lions a 4–0 Test series triumph.

He surely would have been on four Lions' tours but was unavailable for New Zealand in 1977 and South Africa in 1980, which was a pity. He was some talent, one of the greats.

1971. Fergus Slattery shields scrum half Ray Hopkins from the attentions of Bay of Plenty flanker Alan McNaughton.

F. CALDER

Melrose, Stewart's-Melville FP

SCOTLAND

Born 20 August 1957, Haddington
6ft 2in – 15st 6lbs

34 caps for Scotland
first versus France 1986
last versus New Zealand 1991

British Lions – 1 tour, 3 Tests
1989 – Australia (1,2,3)

OPEN SIDE

To have become the only British Lions' captain to win a Test series this century after having lost the first Test had to be one big highlight in the career of Finlay Calder of Stewart's-Melville FP in Edinburgh. His leadership was an important ingredient as the Lions in Australia 1989 won the second and third Tests and so the series.

His participation in that tour also represented a milestone as he followed his brother Jim as a British Lions' Test player, the only twins ever to achieve that feat. Jim had played for the Lions against New Zealand in the third Test of the 1983 tour. The twins had represented Scottish Schools together out of Stewart's-Melville College and against France, Wales and England in 1974-75 (their brother, John, had captained Scottish Schools). Then they set another mark, as Jim was in Scotland's Grand Slam-winning side of 1986 and Finlay followed suit in 1990. There were, in fact, four Calder brothers, all of whom played for Scottish Schools and Stewart's-Melville FP and of whom John joined Finlay and Jim on the Scottish tour to Australia in 1982.

Finlay Calder actually succeeded twin Jim as Scottish flanker. Jim had already gained his 27 caps before Finlay became one of six new caps, among them the Hastings brothers, Gavin and Scott, who breathed new life into the Scottish effort with an 18–17 win over France at Murrayfield on 18 January 1986. Finlay Calder then played 19 cap internationals in a row and by the end of his international career had played in 34 of the preceding 41 cap internationals.

He was a rugged, raw-boned New Zealand type of loose forward who revelled in contact, who had impressive mobility about the pitch, singular strength of character, determination and a refusal to be overawed by any opposition. His handling was of quality too, as he showed notably as a member (with his twin, Jim) of the Stewart's-Melville FP side who won the Middlesex Sevens in 1982 with a 34–12 margin over Richmond in the final. It was typical of Calder's aggressive approach that in the opening joust against England in the Grand Slam decider at Murrayfield on 17 March 1990 he smashed forward into English ranks to create a target for a thundering charge by the entire Scottish pack that set the tone of Scottish defiance and endeavour towards their unexpected 13–7 win. The famous Welsh lock, Brian Price, rated Calder on that day as 'the best player afield'.

At club level Calder had five seasons with Melrose when his work as a grain shipper took him to the Borders, but he gave many years to Stewart's-Melville FP and enjoyed some admirable seven-a-side successes with the club during the eighties.

He played for Scotland in the World Cups of 1987 and 1991 in nine of the 10 games, missing only the Zimbabwe match at Murrayfield in 1991, and he scored tries against Wales at Cardiff on 20 February 1988, France at Murrayfield in the 21–0 win on 17 February 1990 and against the Barbarians in the 16–16 draw on 7 September 1991. He followed another Stewart's-Melville stalwart, Douglas Morgan, as captain of Scotland against Wales, England, Ireland and France in 1989 when Scotland lost only to France. On 30 occasions Finlay Calder and John Jeffrey (Kelso) were Scotland's flankers and they formed a strong breakaway alliance with Derek White (Gala and London Scottish) in 17 cap internationals.

As captain of the 1989 Lions in Australia, Calder demonstrated motivational powers that, according to the *Rothmans Rugby Yearbook* report, 'kept the Lions on the boil and he came through strongly in the final Test when he was one of the players of the match. The Lions' tackling, notably that of Calder and Scott Hastings, especially when Australia came within a point in the final Test, cut Australians down time and again as the Lions held on'. Calder played in six of the 12 games of which only one was lost, the first Test.

Two years later against New Zealand at Cardiff in the third and fourth place play-off in the World Cup Calder rang down the curtain on his international career at 34 years of age, a career rich in endeavour and merited success.

1989. Finlay Calder leading from the front in the first Test in Sydney.

P.J. WINTERBOTTOM

Headingley, Harlequins

ENGLAND

**Born 31 May 1960, Horsforth
6ft – 14st 10lbs**

58 caps for England
first versus Australia 1982
last versus Ireland 1993

British Lions – 2 tours, 7 Tests
1983 – New Zealand (1,2,3,4)
1993 – New Zealand (1,2,3)

OPEN SIDE

It isn't often that a player from the United Kingdom is voted one of the 'players of the year' in New Zealand but that was the honour and compliment paid to Peter James Winterbottom of the Fleetwood, Exeter, Headingley and Harlequins clubs after his deeds of derring-do with the Lions in New Zealand in 1983. He was well acquainted with deeds of derring-do as one of the finest open side flankers the game has seen – strong, determined, totally committed, a scourge of opposing mid-field backs, a crunching tackler, a kind of blonde bomber likened by some to Frenchman Jean-Pierre Rives but harder and more vigorous if not quite as dexterous. Peter Winterbottom wasn't likely to use 10 words if five would do and he let his dynamic style of play do most of his talking for him.

He currently lies sixth in England's caps list after Rory Underwood (85 caps), Will Carling (72), Rob Andrew (71), Brian Moore (64) and Jason Leonard (63). He is also fourth in the

world list of most capped flankers behind Fergus Slattery (61), Jean-Pierre Rives (59) and Simon Poidevin (59).

Winterbottom was educated at Rossall School, Fleetwood, where he benefited from the coaching of John Dewhurst. Then he played for the local club, then for Exeter when a student at Seale-Hayne Agricultural College in Devon. His family had strong ties with the Headingley club of which his father was president and it gave immense pride to Headingley that Peter was playing for them when first capped and when he became a 1983 British Lion in New Zealand. He moved to London in 1989 and joined Harlequins whom he eventually captained. In his early days his handling wasn't quite polished and dependable enough but that it improved with practice and confidence was illustrated by his appearance in Harlequins' sides that contested the Middlesex Sevens final in 1989, 1990 and 1991. They won the first two and were runners-up to London Scottish in the third. Winterbottom captained them in the 1990 and 1991 events.

He made a meteoric leap into the England side via the England Colts against Wales and France as a number eight in 1980, a member of the Yorkshire side in 1981, membership of the England B team against France in 1981 and a first cap in victory by 15–11 over the touring Wallabies at Twickenham in 1982. He just missed a debut cap try in that match after charging down a kick.

He broadened his experience by playing a 1982 season with the Napier Club in Hawke's Bay in New Zealand and also with the Durban Old Boys in South Africa in 1989. He was in the Northern

Grand Slams in 1991 and 1992, and in the World Cup tournaments of 1987 and 1991 he appeared in nine of the 10 games. When England toured South Africa in 1984 the two Tests were lost, 15–33 and 6–38 but following the first, Winterbottom was rated as being 'England's hero, tackling superbly and competing for loose ball against superior numbers'. *Rothmans Rugby Yearbook* also reported that in the second Test 'Winterbottom battled bravely against the odds'.

With the 1983 Lions in New Zealand he played in 12 of 18 games and in all four

1983. Peter Winterbottom makes a break during the second Test in Wellington.

Division championship-winning sides of 1986 and 1987.

It was hardly surprising for one who committed himself without thought for personal wellbeing that occasional injuries interrupted his caps career but from his first appearance against the 1982 Wallabies he played 13 cap internationals on the trot and he played in 29 out of 31 up to his last appearance as a 33-year-old against Ireland in 1993.

He had a key role in all eight games when England gathered in successive

Tests, which were lost, but he showed endurance, aggression and a huge tackle rate. Even in disadvantageous situations Winterbottom never failed to give one hundred per cent as in the 1993 Lions' tour to New Zealand when he played in seven of the 13 games and in all three Tests (lost 2–1) with his English colleagues Ben Clarke (Bath) and Dean Richards (Leicester) as his breakaway partners in all three. That New Zealanders and South Africans alike admired tremendously the Winterbottom style says it all.

T.M. DAVIES

London Welsh, Swansea

WALES

Born 9 December 1946, Swansea
6ft 4 1/2 in – 14st 10lbs

38 caps for Wales
first versus Scotland 1969
last versus France 1976

British Lions – 2 tours, 8 Tests
1971 – Australia/New Zealand (1,2,3,4)
1974 – South Africa (1,2,3,4)

NO. 8

When he first burst upon the international scene he was virtually unknown and given little chance of an international career because he was a long, skinny lad who appeared in need of a good meal! But the doubters were wrong, for Thomas Mervyn Davies, later known to his Welsh following as 'Merv the Swerve', developed into one of the most gifted number eight forwards. He made a huge impression not only at club level but in the red of Wales and of the British Lions. It was no great surprise that Mervyn Davies proved a key figure in arguably the most successful tour ever made by the British Lions – to Australia and New Zealand in 1971, when the Lions won a full Test series in New Zealand for the very first time. Three years later when the 1974 Lions thundered through South Africa for 21 wins and one draw in 22 games played, during which they gave the South Africans their first full-scale lost Test series with three victories and one draw, Davies was influential too.

Mervyn Davies had a gangling look about him but he was athletic with it, a very well-equipped footballer with adhesive hands, a thumping tackle, splendid timing and technique as a number six line-out ball winner (he had played basketball for the Welsh Colleges), and with a long, loping stride that made him awkward to torpedo. There was street wisdom as well but admirable self discipline no matter the provocation. There are many who regard the David Morris, Mervyn Davies and John Taylor trio as the finest loose forward combine ever fielded by Wales: Taylor has written that he never stopped marvelling at the amount of work that Davies got through in a game.

Mervyn Davies qualified as a teacher after attending Penlan School and the College of Education in Swansea. He was on the staff of Emmanuel in Wandsworth and became a stalwart with London Welsh during their halcyon times in the seventies when they put together some marvellously fluent rugby that set the London game alight.

1974. Mervyn Davies, a towering force in both attack and defence in South Africa.

He was part of an all-international breakaway trio at London Welsh with John Taylor and Tony Gray.

He was a shock choice for his first cap against Scotland in 1969, in his first senior season. Another new cap was one J.P.R. Williams. As a chip off the old block (his father played lock for Wales in four 'victory' internationals in 1945-46) Davies established himself in the Welsh side, at one time holding the record as the world's most capped number eight while in his last season of international play he led Wales to their 1976 Grand Slam. His accurate line-out deflections frequently sent his props, notably Graham Price, rumbling round the tail to set up choice ruck ball for the backs and he was a brilliant exponent of the scrummage pick-up. He captained Wales in nine cap internationals as well as two others against Japan and he was virtually an ever present during two Grand Slams, six championships and three Triple Crowns. He would have gained many more caps and might well have captained the British Lions in 1977, but suffered a cerebral haemorrhage in the Welsh cup semi-final in 1976 which ended his career and almost ended his life.

Davies returned to Swansea in 1973, had the honour of being their captain and also captained the Barbarians to their 19–7 win over the Wallabies at Cardiff on 24 January 1976. He had already played for the Barbarians against the 1970 Springboks at Twickenham and in the 13–13 draw with the All Blacks at Twickenham on 30 November 1974 when he was a try scorer.

The Welshman was eminently successful during the 1971 Lions' tour, so outplaying the New Zealanders at the line-out as to bring from the legendary Colin Meads a handsome compliment. He played in 13 of the 26 games including all four Tests and scored three tries. Writing in the *Playfair Rugby Annual*, J.B.G. Thomas referred to Davies as 'doing a notable job at number eight and was quite tireless in attack and defence'.

He was busy in South Africa with the Lions in 1974, playing in 12 of the 22 games, including all four Tests, with Roger Uttley and Fergus Slattery as his loose forward accomplices. Some trio! He scored tries against Eastern Province, South West District, Orange Free State, Northern Transvaal and Natal. Those Lions were fortunate to have two outstanding number eight forwards in Davies and England's Andy Ripley: it was Davies who won the Test spot.

NO. 8

W.P. DUGGAN

Blackrock College

IRELAND

Born 12 March 1950, Kilkenny
6ft 3in – 16st 2lbs

41 caps for Ireland
first versus England 1975
last versus Scotland 1984

British Lions – 1 tour, 4 Tests
1977 – New Zealand (1,2,3,4)

NO. 8

Irish rugby has spawned a rich galaxy of characters whose sometimes outrageous comments or behaviour masked true football ability of the highest class. One such was William Patrick Duggan, whose alleged dislike of training was the butt of much humorous comment but who yet holds the Irish record as their most capped number eight with 39, plus two as a flank forward.

In true Irish style he revelled in tilting his lance with no thought of personal well-being. Initially he had many 'rough edges' but these were smoothed off with experience so that he became a personality liked and respected by friend and foe alike. A big, raw-boned type, he proved to be a rumbustious line-out purveyor and sound in scrummage moves whilst showing a number eight feel for support, linkage and cover. Yet Duggan once delivered at the pithead his profound belief:'I am firmly of the view that the quickest way to take the edge off your form is by training.' Willie always seemed to be last out of the dressing room for training sessions and first back in!

There was a famous occasion, too, at one England versus Ireland international when Duggan, who enjoyed a fag, ran on to Twickenham having forgotten that he still had a lighted cigarette in his hand: he turned and handed it to the touch judge with the request 'Could you look after that for me until half-time?'.

A native of Kilkenny who played in several positions when a pupil at Rockwell College in Tipperary, Duggan first played senior rugby with Sundays Well in Cork before travelling regularly from West Ireland to Dublin to play for Blackrock College in 1972. It was then that his career gained much impetus as he scored the Leinster try in the 9–17 defeat by the 1972 All Blacks and then featured in the Irish trial. He still had three years to wait until his first cap in the 12–9 win over England in Dublin on 18 January 1975. He then played in 18 of the next 19 cap internationals and from 1979 to his last cap appearance in 1984 he gained 18 caps in a row. He played in 10 Five Nations Championships and was a key member of the Irish side who won the championship and Triple Crown in 1982. When Ciaran Fitzgerald (St Mary's College) was injured early in the Welsh game of 1984, Duggan took over as captain and also led his country in the next two matches, against England and Scotland. The contest with Scotland in Dublin was his last cap international, taking place nine days short of his 34th birthday.

Duggan had captained Leinster in 1981 but also played for them in tight games against the touring All Blacks (9–17) on 15 November 1972 (when he scored the Leinster try from number eight) and as flanker in the 3–8 defeat on 13 November 1974. He also was in the Irish side who held Graham Mourie's All Blacks to 6–10, also at Lansdowne Road, on 4 November 1978. He toured with Ireland in New Zealand 1976, Australia 1979 and South Africa 1981, where he took on a

the Wales versus Ireland game at Cardiff on 8 June 1977 he and Geoff Wheel, the Welsh lock, were sent off by Scottish referee Norman Sanson. This proved especially damaging to Irish aspirations because, as one match report stated, 'Duggan had been a key man'. Then in his last cap international when Scotland were going for a Triple Crown at Lansdowne Road on 3 March 1984, the Scots were seeking a scrummage drive-over try when Duggan instinctively dived in to prevent a score. Referee Fred Howard (England) awarded a penalty try and the Scots never looked back. They won 32–9.

With the 1977 Lions in New Zealand Duggan played in 15 of the 26 games including all four Tests. He was the only loose forward to play in all four Tests and scored the only Lions try in their 19–7 defeat in the third Test. Although

1977. Willie Duggan offloads to Terry Cobner in the game against Canterbury.

heavy workload by playing in 16 of the 23 games, including all five Tests. On the tour to New Zealand Duggan had been described as being 'an outstanding figure' in the one international in which the Irish forwards gave a tremendous display but the side failed to make attacking opportunities count and lost by 11–3.

Two major disappointments were experienced by Duggan in his career. In

the Lions lost the series 3–1 their forwards were a formidable combination and Duggan was described as having given 'consistently fine performances throughout the tour'.

There was always fun and dry wit whenever William Patrick Duggan was in the company but he was some player too who, at one time, was the world's most capped number eight.

J. SQUIRE

Newport, Pontypool

WALES

Born 23 September 1951, Newport
6ft 3in – 15st 4lbs

29 caps for Wales
first versus Ireland 1977
last versus France 1983

British Lions – 3 tours, 6 Tests
1977 – New Zealand (4)
1980 – South Africa (1,2,3,4)
1983 – New Zealand (1)

NO. 8

Following in the footsteps of the great Mervyn Davies was always going to be a Herculean task but in his quiet and dedicated manner Jeffrey Squire made his own imprint on the Welsh game. Despite having played in the Davies berth of number eight in his first two internationals, against Ireland and France in 1977, Squire ended up having performed as number eight on eight cap international occasions and as flanker on 22. He was that kind of physically imposing, versatile type who could adapt comfortably to the contrasting tasks of blind side flanker and number eight, a big, rugged fellow who compensated for lack of flaring pace with skill, power and a sharp rugby brain as well as line-out auxiliary dependability and impressive strength in the maul.

A former pupil of Newbridge Grammar School, he extended his rugby education as a student at St Luke's College in Exeter, from where he graduated as a schoolmaster. He was one of a number of St Luke's students who went on to cap status – among them Mike Rafter, John

Scott and Mike Slemen (England) and David Burcher (Wales). His first senior Welsh club experience was with Newport for whom he played in the 7–13 defeat by the touring Australians on 7 January 1976. Newport finished runners-up to Pontypridd in the championship table of that season, scoring over a thousand points and as John Jeffrey, their regular number eight, had left for Blackwood, Squire was described as being 'an outstanding replacement'. In the 1978 Welsh Cup final Squire was in the Newport side who lost to Swansea by only 13–9. He then joined Pontypool and became a member of the most successful pack in Wales whilst also learning more of the trade from an association with Terry Cobner, whom he succeeded as Pontypool captain in the 1979-80 season.

Having replaced the injured Barry Clegg (Swansea) in the non-cap international against the Argentinians in October 1976, Squire gained his first cap against Ireland three months later. He was in rivalry for the number eight berth with Derek Quinnell and it wasn't until the

New Zealand game on 11 November 1978, when Wales lost by only 12–13, that he really established his position in the side by playing in 22 of the next 23 cap internationals, missing only the disaster at Scotland's hands in 1982. He captained Wales on six occasions – throughout the 1980 Five Nations and against Ireland and France in 1981 – and scored tries against England in 1980 and 1983 and against France in 1983.

Squire reacted to Lions duty like a war horse to a bugle. Having been flown out to replace Roger Uttley who sustained back damage in the 1977 Lions squad in New Zealand (and with the Newport club being thrilled to have Squire, Gareth Evans and David Burcher all on the tour), Squire settled to the task of willing work horse, keen to learn and prepared to look the New Zealanders straight in the eye. He played in 14 of the 26 games, scoring tries against King Country, New Zealand juniors and West Coast-Buller and was called in as flanker for the final Test in Auckland which the Lions lost by only 9–10. Squire returned from the tour a more rounded player. When on tour with the 1980 Lions in South Africa he played in 11 of the 18 games, six as flanker, five as number eight, and played in all four Tests, two as flanker and two as number eight. He scored a try in the 16–9 victory over the 'Blue Bulls' of Northern Transvaal and captained the Lions to a 17–6 win over the Junior Springboks. He was reported to have created a fruitful understanding with the Irish flanker, John O'Driscoll, and to have embraced 'an enormous workrate'.

Having been persuaded by the manager, Willie John McBride, to make himself available for the Lions in New Zealand in 1983 (he and Graham Price being the only survivors from the 1977 tour), Squire played in four of the first five games. He scored two tries in the first match against Wanganui and was captain against the Bay of Plenty, but had wretched luck in the way of shoulder damage so that he played only six games including the first Test. Eventually he was invalided home after being injury-replaced by the Scot, John Beattie, following 25 minutes of the 12th game of the tour against North Auckland. His absence from the remaining three Tests was a huge blow to the Lions: he was that good a player.

1983. Jeff Squire in New Zealand on his third Lions tour – a great workhorse with a prodigious workrate.

D. RICHARDS

Leicester

ENGLAND

Born 11 July 1963, Nuneaton
6ft 4in – 17st 8lbs

48 caps for England
first versus Ireland 1986
last versus Ireland 1996

British Lions – 2 tours, 6 Tests
1989 – Australia (1,2,3)
1993 – New Zealand (1,2,3)

NO. 8

He was a Leicester police officer with the build and strength of a grizzly bear and he proved to be the outstanding England number eight during the eighties. He would have set a record of international appearances that might have stood for ages but for missing 31 internationals, mainly through injuries to shoulder, groin, elbow and ankle but partly through selectorial misjudgment. Dean Richards is the man, although he was more often described as a colossus, renowned for mighty feats of power as well as an intuitive feel that made him an inspirational figure at all levels.

Graham Law of *The Scotsman* described him thus after England's 18–9 win at Murrayfield in 1976: 'Dean Richards revealed his ability to latch on to ricochet line-out ball and did the most to ring fence the Scots in their own half. He would stick out a giant paw, claim rights to the ball and refuse to relinquish it to the opposition.' Richards was tough on the Scots! At Murrayfield on 18 January 1992, the English forwards were struggling and

had even conceded a pushover try to Derek White. When Richards came off the bench to replace the injured Tim Rodber (Northampton), however, the English forwards stepped up a gear and, as one reporter described it, 'stuck close to Richards like iron filings to a magnet'. England won, 25–7!

Richards played for England Schools as lock out of St Martin's Roman Catholic School, then studied at John Cleveland College, Hinckley, before joining the police force. He represented England Under 23 and the British Police, joined Leicester in 1982 after a season with the French club Roanne, and then contributed handsomely to Leicester's successes in 15 seasons with the club, making appearances in five cup finals including the 23–16 win over Harlequins in 1993.

His entry into England cap status was dramatically successful – two pushover tries in the 25–20 win over Ireland in Dublin in 1986 and denied another by the award of a penalty try. He became the world's most capped number eight with 48 such appearances as well as six more Tests with the Lions. He was in the England sides who beat New Zealand 15–9 at Twickenham on 27 November 1993 and South Africa in Pretoria by 32–15 on 4 June 1994.

In his 15 seasons with Leicester Richards played over three hundred games and scored over a hundred tries. Immensely strong, he was never likely to create a sonic boom but was possessed with uncanny anticipation and the gift for, more often than not, being close to the ball. He was also a cunning floor operator. His leadership qualities, too, were underlined as captain of the Midlands Division against the 1992 South Africans and the 1993 New Zealanders.

He played in all three World Cup tournaments in 1987, 1991 and 1995, with 10 appearances in 16 games but surprisingly was left out of the France and Scotland games as well as the final against the Australians in 1991 when England lost 6–12. There are those who rate the Ben Clarke, Richards, Lawrence Dallaglio, loose forward trio of 1996 as the strongest England has ever fielded.

Richards continued his commanding form on two tours with the British Lions. In Australia in 1989 he showed courage and durability whilst revelling in the rough, sometimes bitter, series. Socks down, his whole being epitomised courage and challenge, one report claiming that 'the Lions hard-nosed pack reacted to the brilliance of Paul Ackford, Dean Richards and Mike Teague'. Richards played in six of the 12 games and in all three Tests, won 2–1 by the Lions, and was captain against Australia B.

The 1993 tour to New Zealand wasn't quite as successful. The Lions lost the series 2–1 and the first Test to a Grant Fox penalty goal in injury-time after the Australian referee, Brian Kinsey, had blown against Richards for holding down the tackled player although the ball was coming out on the Lions' side. Richards, however, had a good tour, playing in six of the 13 games, scoring a try against Otago and being in the same breakaway trio in all three Tests – Clarke, Richards and Peter Winterbottom.

A wonderfully loyal stalwart for club, division and country, Richards will always be remembered as one with the strength and acumen to turn a game: a true giant.

1989. Dean Richards, Paul Ackford and Wade Dooley present a wall to the Australians in the second Test at Brisbane.

DREAM LIONS XV

THE FINAL SELECTION

15. J.P.R. WILLIAMS

14. T.G.R. DAVIES
13. C.M.H. GIBSON
12. J.C. GUSCOTT
11. D.J. DUCKHAM

10. B. JOHN
9. G.O. EDWARDS

1. F.E. COTTON
2. P.J. WHEELER
3. G. PRICE

4. W.J. McBRIDE (Capt)
5. G.L. BROWN

6. M.C. TEAGUE
7. J.F. SLATTERY
8. T.M. DAVIES

WE HAVE MAJOR
PLAYERS ON OUR TEAM

HongkongBank

Midland Bank

Hang Seng Bank

Marine Midland Bank

Hongkong Bank of Canada

Banco HSBC Bamerindus

Hongkong Bank Malaysia

The British Bank of the Middle East

HSBC Banco Roberts

HongkongBank of Australia

HSBC Investment Banking

The HSBC Group

Over 5,500 offices in 79 countries and territories

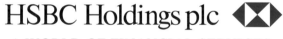

HSBC Holdings plc ◆

A WORLD OF FINANCIAL SERVICES

Issued by HSBC Holdings plc, 10 Lower Thames Street, London EC3R 6AE, United Kingdom

IAN McGEECHAN
on Coaching the Dream Lions

In appraising this team I have made two assumptions:

 (a) that all the players are playing at the peak of their careers, and

 (b) that the team would play in the current era, particularly in the last two years when there have been significant changes in tactics and approach.

What strikes me immediately about the team is the obvious physical and mental strength of the forwards, and the number of backs who are capable of individual brilliance, attributes which are now essential to play a whole team game.

Starting up front, where I believe games are still won and lost, the ability to scrummage aggressively is a massive strength of this pack. They would be able to move a scrum left or right to their advantage in attack, or to the opposition's disadvantage in defence.

My mouth waters at the thought of an attacking scrum coming up on the right hand side and allowing Gareth Edwards a free run into mid-field from the left or down the blind side from the right. With today's laws no one would get near him – he has genuine pace, and pound for pound the strongest upper body of any back. When eventually a tackle comes in he would have the choice of Barry John, Mike Gibson or Jerry Guscott running free off him.

This is the area in which I think this team would be most devastating, i.e. a dominant scrum releasing Mervyn Davies and a group of threequarters into a series of one-on-one situations. It is also worth remembering that once the ball was in open play there are a number of forwards, particularly the front row, who are natural ball-handlers: Fran Cotton, with his rugby league and World Sevens background, Peter Wheeler, a natural passer, and Graham Price, who has the confidence to kick, chase, run and score from 50 metres out in Paris.

Although the overall height of the pack is not great, the current lifting laws make Willie John and Gordon Brown very formidable opponents. Yet only three years ago they would have found life very difficult against the 6ft 10in lighthouses whom we saw dominating the 'pre-lifting' line-outs.

Mervyn Davies is a very important third target man for the thrower, and although neither centre would want to take ball up 'into the traffic' just for the sake of contact, good attacking rules could be achieved with the likes of Fran, Graham Price and Mike Teague running around the back of the line-out. What this would achieve would be the scenario of big forwards getting at the opposition mid-field and the subsequent possession finding Barry John, Mike Gibson, Gerald Davies et al running at the opposing forwards. (For some reason the phrase 'taking the p***' comes to mind.)

Another significant development in the current game is that of tactical kicking, keeping the ball in play, and then pressurising in numbers. Well, firstly, if I had to chose anybody to be under a high ball, anywhere in the world, it would be J.P.R. Williams. Not only does he have tremendous hands but also the strength to stay on his feet when under great pressure; just as important, he has the brain and attitude to run any ball that isn't perfect straight back. The pre-attacking potential of the back three is awesome. So JPR catches and offloads to either David Duckham or Gerald Davies, running at pace in a broken field, providing a lethal cocktail of strength, pace, brilliant side-steps and guile – oh, by the way, the next support player is Jerry Guscott. Say no more, just enjoy the spectacle.

Another overall strength of this team is the innate handling skills from number 9 outwards. This allows any set-piece ball to be taken to any part of the field quickly, and certainly gives JPR and his wingers space wide for one-on-one attacks.

The intelligent hands of the mid-field would also be very important in offloading ball in and out of contact and to allow the likes of Mike Teague to make punishing runs into the heart of a defence.

Even when a kicking strategy needs to be employed, numbers 9, 10, 12 and 13 can all take responsibility for leaving the ball in space, be it via a chip over the defence or a penetrating diagonal behind the wingers. The back line bristles with confidence and decision-makers, who could continuously vary the point of attack – vital in today's game.

Because points of attack do vary and because width can be vital, the pace and non-stop running of Fergus Slattery ensure the first man to the breakdown and thus all the necessary continuity.

The only area for concern would be first-up tackles and contact in the backs, but with the team ethic and single-mindedness invoked by Willie John, you can bet the first tackle, whatever his size, would at least 'keep hold' long enough for the second man to team tackle.

Willie John as captain would give this team not just the confidence but the assured calmness to play. The pack under his leadership would be uncompromising, which is still very important if you have to buy time and space to play. It has the physical edge to challenge at scrum, line-out, ruck and maul. In short, this is a team and a captain to die for.

The real excitement and anticipation would be to see this team with the ball. Its ball-winning capacity is strong and its potential brilliance frightening. Who could ask for more?

1910
Dr Smythe's Lions in South Africa

P24 W13 D3 L8 F290 A236

South Western Districts	W	14	4
Western Province (Country)	W	9	3
Western Province (Colleges)	W	11	3
Western Province (Town)	D	11	11
Western Province	W	5	3
Griqualand West	L	0	8
Transvaal	L	8	27
Pretoria	W	17	0
Transvaal (Country)	L	6	13
Natal	W	18	16
Natal	W	19	13
Orange River Colony	W	12	9
Griqualand West	L	3	9
Cape Colony	L	0	19
Rhodesia	W	24	11
SOUTH AFRICA (Kimberley)	L	10	14
North Eastern Districts	D	8	8
Border	W	30	10
Border	D	13	13
Eastern Province	W	14	6
SOUTH AFRICA (Port Elizabeth)	W	8	3
SOUTH AFRICA (Cape Town)	L	5	21
Western Province	L	0	8

1930
F.D. Prentice's Lions in New Zealand and Australia

P28 W20 L8 D0 F624 A318

Wanganui	W	19	3
Taranaki	W	23	7
Manawhenua	W	34	8
Wairarapa–Bush	W	19	6
Wellington	L	8	12
Canterbury	L	8	14
West Coast–Buller	W	34	11
Otago	W	33	9
NEW ZEALAND (Dunedin)	W	6	3
Southland	W	9	3
Ashburton, South Canterbury and North Otago	W	16	9
NEW ZEALAND (Christchurch)	L	10	13
Maoris	W	19	13
Hawke's Bay	W	14	3
East Coast, Poverty Bay and Bay of Plenty	W	25	11
Auckland	L	6	19
NEW ZEALAND (Auckland)	L	10	15
North Auckland	W	38	5
Waikato, Thames Valley and King Country	W	40	16
NEW ZEALAND (Wellington)	L	8	22

Marlborough, Nelson and Golden Bay	W	41	3
New South Wales	W	29	10
AUSTRALIA (Sydney)	L	5	6
Queensland	W	26	16
Australian XV	W	29	14
New South Wales	L	3	28
Victoria	W	41	36
Western Australia (unofficial)	W	71	3

1938
Sammy Walker's Lions in South Africa

P24 W17 L7 D0 F414 A284

Border	W	11	8
Griqualand West	W	22	9
Western Province (Town and Country)	L	8	11
South Western Districts	W	19	10
Western Province	L	11	21
Western Transvaal	W	26	9
Orange Free State	W	21	6
Orange Free State (Country)	W	18	3
Transvaal	L	9	16
Northern Transvaal	W	20	12
Cape Province	W	10	3
Rhodesia	W	25	11
Rhodesia	W	45	11
Transvaal	W	17	9
SOUTH AFRICA (Johannesburg)	L	12	26
Northern Province	L	8	26
Natal	W	15	11
Border	W	19	11
North Eastern Districts	W	42	3
Eastern Province	W	6	5
SOUTH AFRICA (Port Elizabeth)	L	3	19
SOUTH AFRICA (Cape Town)	W	21	16
Combined Universities	W	19	16
Western Province (unofficial)	L	7	12

1950
Karl Mullen's Lions in New Zealand and Australia

P30 W23 D1 L6 F614 A220

Nelson, Marlborough, Golden Bay and Motueka	W	24	3
Buller	W	24	9
West Coast	W	32	3
Otago	L	9	23
Southland	L	0	11
NEW ZEALAND (Dunedin)	D	9	9
South Canterbury	W	27	8
Canterbury	W	16	5
Ashburton County–North Otago	W	29	6

NEW ZEALAND (Christchurch)	L	0	8
Wairarapa–Bush	W	27	13
Hawke's Bay	W	20	0
East Coast, Poverty Bay and Bay of Plenty	W	27	3
Wellington	W	12	6
NEW ZEALAND (Wellington)	L	3	6
Wanganui	W	31	3
Taranaki	W	25	3
Manawatu–Horowhenua	W	13	8
Waikato, Thames Valley and King Country	W	30	0
North Auckland	W	8	6
Auckland	W	32	9
NEW ZEALAND (Auckland)	L	8	11
New Zealand Maoris	W	14	9

Combined Country	W	47	3
New South Wales	W	22	6
AUSTRALIA (Brisbane)	W	19	6
AUSTRALIA (Sydney)	W	24	3
Metropolitan Union	W	26	17
New South Wales XV	L	12	17

Ceylon (unofficial)	W	44	6

1955
Robin Thompson's Lions in South Africa

P25 W19 D1 L5 F457 A283

Western Transvaal	L	6	9
Griqualand West	W	24	14
Northern Universities	W	32	6
Orange Free State	W	31	3
South West Africa	W	9	0
Western Province	W	11	3
South Western Districts	W	22	3
Eastern Province	L	0	20
North Eastern Districts	W	34	6
Transvaal	W	36	13
Rhodesia	W	27	14
Rhodesia	W	16	12
SOUTH AFRICA (Johannesburg)	W	23	22
Central Universities	W	21	14
Boland	W	11	0
Western Province Universities	W	20	17
SOUTH AFRICA (Cape Town)	L	9	25
Eastern Transvaal	D	17	17
Northern Transvaal	W	14	11
SOUTH AFRICA (Pretoria)	W	9	6
Natal	W	11	8
Junior Springboks	W	15	12
Border	L	12	14
SOUTH AFRICA (Port Elizabeth)	L	8	22

East African XV	W	39	12

Unisys and Rugby

To us it's not just a game

Unisys is an information technology solutions provider with a portfolio of information services, technologies and third party alliances enabling us to help clients make the most of their information assets.

We are proud to have been associated with world class rugby for ten years providing statistical information and results services for the written press, radio and TV.

In addition to our match results and broadcast services we are also involved with the day to day running of the Rugby Football Union (RFU) player registration scheme, the National Results service, the youth registration scheme and general computing services at the Twickenham headquarters.

Visit the Unisys Sports Systems website to find out more: www.unisys.com/sports

1959
Ronnie Dawson's Lions in Australia, New Zealand and Canada

P33 W27 D0 L6 F842 A353

Victoria	W	53	18
New South Wales	L	14	18
Queensland	W	39	11
AUSTRALIA (Brisbane)	W	17	6
New South Wales Country Districts	W	27	14
AUSTRALIA (Sydney)	W	24	3

Hawke's Bay	W	52	12
East Coast–Poverty Bay	W	23	14
Auckland	W	15	10
New Zealand Universities	W	25	13
Otago	L	8	26
South Canterbury, North Otago and Mid-Canterbury	W	21	11
Southland	W	11	6
NEW ZEALAND (Dunedin)	L	17	18
West Coast–Buller	W	58	3
Canterbury	L	14	20
Marlborough, Nelson, Golden Bay and Montueka	W	64	5
Wellington	W	21	6
Wanganui	W	9	6
Taranaki	W	15	3
Manawatu–Horowhenua	W	26	6
NEW ZEALAND (Wellington)	L	8	11
King Country–Counties	W	25	5
Waikato	W	14	0
Wairarapa–Bush	W	37	11
NEW ZEALAND (Christchurch)	L	8	22
New Zealand Juniors	W	29	9
New Zealand Maoris	W	12	6
Thames Valley–Bay of Plenty	W	26	24
North Auckland	W	35	13
NEW ZEALAND (Auckland)	W	9	6

British Columbia	W	16	11
Eastern Canada	W	70	6

1962
Arthur Smith's Lions in South Africa

P25 W16 D4 L5 F401 A208

Rhodesia	W	38	9
Griqualand West	D	8	8
Western Transvaal	W	11	6
Southern Universities	W	14	11
Boland	W	25	8
South West Africa	W	14	6
Northern Transvaal	L	6	14
SOUTH AFRICA (Johannesburg)	D	3	3
Natal	W	13	3
Eastern Province	W	21	6
Orange Free State	D	14	14
Junior Springboks	W	16	11
Combined Services	W	20	6
Western Province	W	21	13
South Western Districts	W	11	3
SOUTH AFRICA (Durban)	L	0	3
Northern Universities	D	6	6
Transvaal	W	24	3
SOUTH AFRICA (Cape Town)	L	3	8
North Eastern Districts	W	34	8
Border	W	5	0
Central Universities	W	14	6
Eastern Transvaal	L	16	19
SOUTH AFRICA (Bloemfontein)	L	14	34

East Africa	W	50	0

1966
Mike Campbell-Lamerton's Lions in Australia, New Zealand and Canada

P35 W23 D3 L9 F524 A345

Western Australia	W	60	3
South Australia	W	38	11
Victoria	W	24	14
Combined Country XV	W	6	3
New South Wales	D	6	6
AUSTRALIA (Sydney)	W	11	8
Queensland	W	26	3
AUSTRALIA (Brisbane)	W	31	0

Southland	L	8	14
South Canterbury, North Otago and Mid Canterbury	W	20	12
Otago	L	9	17
New Zealand Universities	W	24	11
Wellington	L	6	20
Marlborough, Nelson, Golden Bay and Motueka	W	22	14
Taranaki	W	12	9
Bay of Plenty	D	6	6
North Auckland	W	6	3
NEW ZEALAND (Dunedin)	L	3	20
West Coast–Buller	W	25	6
Canterbury	W	8	6
Manawatu–Horowhenua	W	17	8
Auckland	W	12	6
Wairarapa–Bush	W	9	6
NEW ZEALAND (Wellington)	L	12	16
Wanganui–King Country	L	6	12
New Zealand Maoris	W	16	14
East Coast–Poverty Bay	W	9	6
Hawke's Bay	D	11	11
NEW ZEALAND (Christchurch)	L	6	19
New Zealand Juniors	W	9	3
Waikato	W	20	9
Thames Valley–Counties	W	13	9
NEW ZEALAND (Auckland)	L	11	24

British Columbia	L	3	8
Canada (Toronto)	W	19	8

1968
Tom Kiernan's Lions in South Africa

P20 W15 D1 L4 F377 A181

Western Transvaal	W	20	12
Western Province	W	10	6
South Western Districts	W	24	6
Eastern Province	W	23	14
Natal	W	17	5
Rhodesia	W	32	6
SOUTH AFRICA (Pretoria)	L	20	25
North West Cape	W	25	5
South West Africa	W	23	0
Transvaal	L	6	14
SOUTH AFRICA (Port Elizabeth)	D	6	6
Eastern Transvaal	W	37	9
Northern Transvaal	W	22	19
Griqualand West	W	11	3
Boland	W	14	0
SOUTH AFRICA (Cape Town)	L	6	11
Border	W	26	6
Orange Free State	W	9	3
North East Cape	W	40	12
SOUTH AFRICA (Johannesburg)	L	6	19

1971
John Dawes's Lions in Australia and New Zealand

P26 W23 D1 L2 F580 A231

Queensland	L	11	15
New South Wales	W	14	12

Counties–Thames Valley	W	25	3
King Country–Wanganui	W	22	9
Waikato	W	35	14
New Zealand Maoris	W	23	12
Wellington	W	47	9
South Canterbury–North Otago	W	25	6
Otago	W	21	9
West Coast–Buller	W	39	6
Canterbury	W	14	3
Marlborough–Nelson	W	31	12
NEW ZEALAND (Dunedin)	W	9	3
Southland	W	25	3
Taranaki	W	14	9
New Zealand Universities	W	27	6
NEW ZEALAND (Christchurch)	L	12	22

It's good to talk.

Here's to many more years of talking about the British Lions' success

For further information about BT visit www.bt.com

Wairarapa–Bush	W	27	6
Hawke's Bay	W	25	6
East Coast–Poverty Bay	W	18	12
Auckland	W	19	12
NEW ZEALAND (Wellington)	W	13	3
Manawatu–Horowhenua	W	39	6
North Auckland	W	11	5
Bay of Plenty	W	20	14
NEW ZEALAND (Auckland)	D	14	14

1974
Willie John McBride's Lions in South Africa

P22   W21   D1   L0   F729   A207

Western Transvaal	W	59	13
South West Africa	W	23	16
Boland	W	33	6
Eastern Province	W	28	14
South Western Districts	W	97	0
Western Province	W	17	8
SAR Federation XV	W	37	6
SOUTH AFRICA (Cape Town)	W	12	3
Southern Universities	W	26	4
Transvaal	W	23	15
Rhodesia	W	42	6
SOUTH AFRICA (Pretoria)	W	28	9
Quaggas	W	20	16
Orange Free State	W	11	9
Griqualand West	W	69	16
Northern Transvaal	W	16	12
Leopards	W	56	10
SOUTH AFRICA (Port Elizabeth)	W	26	9
Border	W	26	6
Natal	W	34	6
Eastern Transvaal	W	33	10
SOUTH AFRICA (Johannesburg)	D	13	13

1977
Phil Bennett's Lions in New Zealand and Fiji

P26   W21   D0   L5   F607   A320

Wairarapa–Bush	W	41	13
Hawke's Bay	W	13	11
Poverty Bay–East Coast	W	25	6
Taranaki	W	21	13
King Country–Wanganui	W	60	9
Manawatu–Horowhenua	W	18	12
Otago	W	12	7
Southland	W	20	12
New Zealand Universities	L	9	21
NEW ZEALAND (Wellington)	L	12	16
Hanan Shield Districts	W	45	6
Canterbury	W	14	13
West Coast–Buller	W	45	0
Wellington	W	13	6

Marlborough–Nelson	W	40	23
NEW ZEALAND (Christchurch)	W	13	9
New Zealand Maoris	W	22	19
Waikato	W	18	13
New Zealand Juniors	W	19	9
Auckland	W	34	15
NEW ZEALAND (Dunedin)	L	7	19
Counties-Thames Valley	W	35	10
North Auckland	W	18	7
Bay of Plenty	W	23	16
NEW ZEALAND (Auckland)	L	9	10
Fiji	L	21	25

1980
Bill Beaumont's Lions in South Africa

P18   W15   D0   L3   F401   A244

Eastern Province	W	28	16
SARA Invitation XV	W	28	6
Natal	W	21	15
SA Invitation XV	W	22	19
Orange Free State	W	21	17
SAR Federation XV	W	15	6
SOUTH AFRICA (Cape Town)	L	22	26
SA Country Districts	W	27	7
Transvaal	W	32	12
Eastern Transvaal	W	21	15
SOUTH AFRICA (Bloemfontein)	L	19	26
Junior Springboks	W	17	6
Northern Transvaal	W	16	9
SOUTH AFRICA (Port Elizabeth)	L	10	12
SA Barbarians	W	25	14
Western Province	W	37	6
Griqualand West	W	23	19
SOUTH AFRICA (Pretoria)	W	17	13

1983
Ciaran Fitzgerald's Lions in New Zealand

P18   W12   D0   L6   F478   A276

Wanganui	W	47	15
Auckland	L	12	13
Bay of Plenty	W	34	16
Wellington	W	27	19
Manawatu	W	25	18
Mid Canterbury	W	26	6
NEW ZEALAND (Christchurch)	L	12	16
West Coast–Buller	W	52	16
Southland	W	41	3
Wairarapa–Bush	W	57	10
NEW ZEALAND (Wellington)	L	0	9
North Auckland	W	21	12
Canterbury	L	20	22
NEW ZEALAND (Dunedin)	L	8	15
Hawke's Bay	W	25	19

Counties	W	25	16
Waikato	W	40	13
NEW ZEALAND (Auckland)	L	6	38

1989
Finlay Calder's Lions in Australia

P12   W11   D0   L1   F360   A182

Western Australia	W	44	0
Australia B	W	23	8
Queensland	W	19	15
Queensland B	W	30	6
New South Wales	W	23	21
New South Wales B	W	39	19
AUSTRALIA (Sydney)	L	12	30
ACT	W	41	25
AUSTRALIA (Brisbane)	W	19	12
AUSTRALIA (Sydney)	W	19	18
NSW Country	W	72	13
ANZAC XV	W	19	15

1993
Gavin Hastings's Lions in New Zealand

P13   W7   D0   L6   F314   A285

North Auckland	W	30	17
North Harbour	W	29	13
New Zealand Maoris	W	24	20
Canterbury	W	28	10
Otago	L	24	37
Southland	W	34	16
NEW ZEALAND (Christchurch)	L	18	20
Taranaki	W	49	25
Auckland	L	18	23
Hawke's Bay	L	17	29
NEW ZEALAND (Wellington)	W	20	7
Waikato	L	10	38
NEW ZEALAND (Auckland)	L	13	30

1997
Martin Johnson's Lions in South Africa

P13   W11   D0   L2   F480   A278

Eastern Province	W	39	11
Border	W	18	14
Western Province	W	38	21
Mpumalanga	W	64	14
Northern Transvaal	L	30	35
Gauteng	W	20	14
Natal	W	42	12
Emerging Springboks	W	51	22
SOUTH AFRICA (Cape Town)	W	25	16
Free State	W	52	30
SOUTH AFRICA (Durban)	W	18	15
Northern Free State	W	67	39
SOUTH AFRICA (Johannesburg)	L	16	35

WHEN IT COMES TO SELLING YOUR HOME WE WON'T LEAVE YOU HIGH AND DRY

Photograph supplied by Newcastle Falcons

For your local office Tel:–0191 226 1133

As you step into the hurley burley of the property market you will want to know that you are not the only one who's keeping their eye on the ball. You also want to know that you have the backing of a great team. And who better than General Accident Property Services to provide all the support you need. Backed by one of the most respected insurance companies General Accident, the property division enjoys an equally reliable and trusted reputation.

First of all we will give you, without obligation, a FREE market appraisal followed by sound, practical, advice and you'll get the same unstinting commitment and service whether you are looking to sell a one-bedroom flat or a country estate. And with literally hundreds of buyers on our books you won't have to wait too long. When the time comes for you to choose an Estate Agent make sure you select General Accident.

GA

General Accident Property Services